ALLIE
DUNBA

MONEY GUIDES

CW01072875

BUYING YOUR HOME

BUYING YOUR HOME

Richard Newell

© Allied Dunbar Financial Services Limited 1988

ISBN 0–85121–379–0

Published by

Longman Professional and Business Communications Division
Longman Group UK Limited
21–27 Lamb's Conduit Street, London WC1N 3NJ

Associated Offices

Australia   Longman Professional Publishing (Pty) Limited
130 Phillip Street, Sydney, NSW 2000

Hong Kong   Longman Group (Far East) Limited
Cornwall House, 18th Floor, Taikoo Trading Estate,
Tong Chong Street, Quarry Bay

Malaysia   Longman Malaysia Sdn Bhd
No 3 Jalan Kilang A, Off Jalan Penchala,
Petaling Jaya, Selangor, Malysia

Singapore   Longman Singapore Publishers (Pte) Ltd
25 First Lok Yang Road, Singapore 2262

USA   Longman Group (USA) Inc
500 North Dearborn Street, Chicago, Illinois 60610

A CIP catalogue record for this book is available from the British Library.

Printed in Great Britain by Biddles Ltd, Guildford, Surrey.

Richard Newell

Richard Newell is a freelance journalist with ten years experience covering financial matters for national newspapers and magazines.

During this time, he has been editor of *Money Magazine*, editor of *Insurance Age* and assistant editor of *Money Management*.

He has also written for *The Times*, *The Financial Times*, *The Independent* and *Today*. The magazines he writes for include *Family Wealth* and *Planned Savings*. Richard is currently 'living in sin' in North London.

Introduction

Despite the prohibitive cost of property in some parts of the country, home buying is as popular as it has ever been. Over 62% of the population now own their own home. For first time buyers, the average cost ranges from £22,000 in Yorkshire to £61,000 in and around London. As a growth investment with limited risk, property is second to none. It has been estimated that over the last 12 years, prices in the south of England have risen by 400%, while in other parts of the country the average has been 250%.

Buying property is not necessarily straightforward. Reading this book will not only familiarise you with the standard house buying procedure, it will also prepare you for the untoward things that can happen. Your friends and relatives may have told you of their problematic and expensive house-buying experiences. You may already have taken the plunge yourself and found it intimidating. But it needn't be this way. Buying your home is a major investment of time and money on your part and the best way to protect your interests is to be as aware of the short cuts and pitfalls as possible.

You will have to learn as you go to a certain extent because nothing can match real experience of house buying. But reading this book should give you the confidence you need to get a good deal for your money, rather than having to settle simply for what you are offered. To secure the home you want, you must be able to make a quick decision but you must also show patience as the process unfolds. *Buying Your Home* is designed to guide you through the process, from start to finish.

I would like to acknowledge the assistance provided by Keith Boddy of Tomkins Boddy & Co. who vetted the chapter on solicitors and conveyancing and Ian Moffett of Dundas and Wilson who kindly helped out with the description of the conveyancing system in Scotland. Thanks also to Andy Couchman at Allied Dunbar for the mortgage illustrations and to Clifford Green and David Vessey, the Allied Dunbar publishing duo for their time and help.

As regards the unreasonable assumption that all housebuyers, estate agents, solicitors, landlords and building society managers are men, I would quote from my own lease the following gobbledegook:

Words importing the masculine gender shall be deemed to include the feminine and neuter gender and words in the singular shall include the plural and vice versa and where two or more persons are included from time to time in the expression 'the lessor' and 'the lessee' covenants entered into or made or accepted by such persons shall be deemed to be contracted jointly and severally and to be performed accordingly.

This edition incorporates all the relevant changes announced in the 1988 Budget.

Richard Newell
April 1988

Contents

1 Your first steps

'Anyone who buys property is virtually guaranteed to make a profit.' It's not a written guarantee, and it's probably tempting providence to say so. But the fact is that apart from the occasional hiccup property has historically been a secure investment. Stock markets and economic cycles may fluctuate, but property remains as safe as ever.

How much can you afford?

The urge to buy is particularly acute when it comes to property. First time buyers often suffer what has been described as 'the fever', but it also afflicts experienced and otherwise rational people. In the feverish state, prospective buyers can convince themselves of anything – that they can afford to take on a loan of four times their salary, in addition to car loan repayments, a hefty service charge on their 'dream' flat, and fares to work. Sometimes they are assisted in this delusion by their friends, and by estate agents who say they know someone who will lend them what they need.

The moral of this tale is don't bite off more than you can chew. Buying a home is often seen as just one item in our busy lives whereas the reality is that it is likely to be the biggest financial transaction that we ever undertake. Consequently, it needs careful consideration and all aspects of buying your new home should be put into the context of your overall financial planning.

A new (or larger) house doesn't just mean additional mortgage payments. Your house has to be insured and you will want to insure it for its full rebuilding cost. Your contents will need to be insured (and if you're moving to a larger house you may well find you need bigger insurance premiums to cover those extra carpets and extra curtains). Your lender will also want to know that you've got adequate life assurance – for his protection, not yours.

Don't budget *too* carefully

It's important that your budget isn't too finely tuned because it won't take too much to knock you off course. If your budget is close to breaking point most of the time, all it will take to burst your bubble is for interest rates to rise and you won't be able to meet the mortgage repayments without cutting back somewhere else. The best way to avoid getting into any kind of mess is to plan ahead. The following example shows the incidental costs of buying a house for £75,000. The fees are approximate and can vary widely, so shop around for cheap estimates.

	£
Building society's valuation	200
Independent surveyor's report	250
Solicitor's fee (say, ½% inclusive of VAT)	375
Stamp Duty (1%)	750
Land Registry fee	200
Local land charges search fee	15
Central land charges search fee	1
	1,791

Add to this your other immediate costs:

	£
Ground rent	50
Property contents insurance	350
Removal costs	150
Total	2,341

Then, of course, you will have your normal living costs, food, fares, etc. And last but not least, there is the monthly mortgage payment. Most lenders realise that money is tight when you first move in, and they will not usually expect the first payment until the month after you take possession.

Use the example above as an overall guide to find out whether or not your budget is going to be able to take the strain. The idea is to get yourself into the habit of managing your money more efficiently and this will give you a much clearer idea of how much money you really have to spare on a monthly basis.

One tip which a number of people overlook is to try and avoid carrying over extra debts into your new home. You may have a number of small debts spread over a number of sources (credit and store cards for example) so ask your bank to give you a loan so that you can pay them all off. Then you will only have to pay off one debt and a cheaper one at that. The interest on the bank loan may only be 2% above base rate, whereas credit cards and store cards charge anything from 20 to 35% annual interest.

Moving house can be expensive enough and there will always be the sudden and unexpected extra expenses which crop up, not unnaturally, when you least expect them. Keeping your debts under control is an important part of your financial planning, particularly when you're buying a home. You will find some more thoughts on your financial planning in Chapter 6.

Looking at property

Finding the right property means doing the ground work: getting out and seeing the standard of property for sale in your chosen area, then seeking out the bargains. If you do your research, you will soon be able to assess properties quickly and make a decision one way or the other. If you don't research the market, you risk paying over the odds for a property you are not entirely happy with.

You should, of course, first do some research on yourself. What kind of property do you want to live in? How near to the shops? How near to schools? Unimportant points now, perhaps, but what happens in two or three years' time when a baby arrives? How does its location fit in with your job? You may have to travel to London each day by train but drawing a train travel map by *time* from London might produce some locations you hadn't originally thought of. Being within ten miles of a motorway junction could make all the difference regardless of whether you work in Bristol or Edinburgh.

A large, 'well-tended' garden may look great but it has to be kept 'well-tended'. Those windows with the tiny panes may look really attractive as the sun falls on them but they are going to need repainting particularly if the sun falls on them for any period of time. (We tend to forget in this frequently gloomy climate of ours that south-facing paintwork has to cope with a huge range of temperatures from as low as 0°F in the winter to over 100° in the summer.

Chapter 12 contains a checklist of the sort of things you should bear in mind and that might be overlooked in your eagerness to buy. Above all, be prepared to compromise – look for the house that fits your requirements in the major ways. You can always repaint the dining room or replace an old bathroom suite.

Older property

You may be interested in buying an older property which needs improving but is therefore selling at a good price. If this is the case, make sure you fully realise the extent of the work which needs to be undertaken and that it is within your ability both to carry out and to afford the work.

Many older properties are 'listed' by the Department of the Environment as buildings of historical value. You or your solicitor can find out from the local District Council if this is the case.

Depending upon the extent of the renovations or alterations you are considering, you may need planning permission from the council in order to be allowed to carry them out. In the case of listed properties, the council are likely to insist upon high quality of materials and workmanship which will most likely add to the cost for which you had budgeted. However, under these circumstances there are often council grants available for improvements and grant-giving bodies who will contribute towards the additional cost of improvements owing to the property being listed. The local council will know of these organisations, but an enquiry to your local Civic Society might also prove useful.

Flats

You may not be considering buying a whole property but are looking for a flat. The buying process is the same as for a house except that you rarely buy the freehold to the land.

Most modern flats are sold on the basis of a long leasehold tenure for the building, but with the grounds being run by a management company to which each flat owner must pay a regular fee as a contribution to the upkeep of the grounds. You should look carefully at how 'open-ended' the management fee agreement is before you sign it. Consult your solicitor and talk to existing flat owners.

Similarly, there may be a separate maintenance scheme for repairs to the fabric of the building. In some cases, this may also be handled by the grounds management company. Again, study their agreement carefully before you sign. These costs will not be trivial in your calculations when assessing how much you can afford to pay for your flat.

The questions to ask

Compile a list of questions to ask at each place you visit. Ask questions like 'Is the property freehold or leasehold?' Most houses are freehold while most flats are leasehold. A freehold property is one that you own outright, with no landlord to answer to. It could therefore be worth more than a leasehold property, which is one where you are the owner for the term of the lease only.

If a property is leasehold, ask 'How long does the lease have to run?' If the answer is more than 75 years, that's good. Most lenders will think twice about lending on a short lease because it can hinder the resale value. Strictly speaking, a short lease is one with less than 20 years to run, but from a lender's point of view, anything less than 50 years may be unacceptable particularly for a long term loan. It is possible you may have the option of buying the freehold, which will allow you to renegotiate the length of the lease. If so, the seller is bound to point this out because it's a strong selling point.

Other questions to ask include:

- How much is the annual rates bill?
- What are the annual service charges (leasehold only)?
- Has there been any major structural repair recently?
- Are there any building work payments outstandings from this?
- What fixtures and fittings are you leaving?
- Are these included in the price?

It is a good idea to ask the owners how quickly they can move. This is especially important if you are involved in a chain of buying and selling.

Getting your loan sorted out

Building societies and banks have traditionally only allowed mortgage loans of two and a half times your salary, plus one times your partner's if there are two of you buying. That is their considered opinion, based on years of lending experience, of how much a mortgage the average person can afford to take on. But in recent years, as other lenders have entered the market with more attractive terms, the traditional lenders have become more flexible. If you are in a secure, well-paid job you can now raise three times your salary, plus one or maybe one and a half times your partner's. Some lenders even offer up to two and a half times *joint* salaries. Not everyone necessarily has a well paid job, particularly those trying to buy a house for the first time. What you may have to do, therefore, is to shop around to see if you can find slightly better deals that will enable you to get a foot on the housing ladder.

Guarantor mortgage

One possible approach is a guarantor mortgage. This is particularly useful if you're finding it difficult to get a mortgage because of a relatively low income but where you have a parent who is better-off and who is in a position to guarantee the interest payments on your own loan. The multiple that you can borrow is then based on the salary of whoever is the guarantor with the ultimate penalty for them, of course, being that if you default on your repayments, they have to pay.

A *few* lenders undertake this kind of mortgage. It is rather more time consuming as far as they are concerned because they will be looking at the credit position not only of yourself but also of your guarantor. You can expect the lender to take a very careful interest in your guarantor's overall financial position because naturally they will not wish to expose themselves to a loan that could be defaulted upon because the guarantor is unable to make the payments.

Higher multiple mortgage

Another possibility is a higher multiple mortgage. Once again, if you shop around, you may find some lenders who are prepared to lend you more than three times your income and some lenders go as high as four times. Here too they're going to look very carefully at your overall financial position and there will be a tendency for these lenders to lend on higher multiples to people who they feel have a good financial future so that the multiple effectively drops to a more comfortable level in a fairly short space of time.

Low-start mortgage

Another alternative (and these are not necessarily restricted to first-time buyers) is the low-start mortgage. These mortgages are based on paying a lower level of interest at the start and adding the 'missed' interest payments onto the capital so that the later payments increase. Within that very simple structure, there is a range of possibilities and it's not at all uncommon for low-start mortgages to be geared to individual requirements. For example:

1   It's possible to start paying at a 30% discount on the level of interest and to gradually increase your total monthly repayments over a period of time. This could mean that your payments increase by small amounts each year over the whole term of the mortgage.
2   Alternatively, it would be possible to pay a reduced level of interest on a level basis for a certain number of years and then to increase the repayments up to a higher level for the remainder of the mortgage term.
3   It would also be possible to start paying a lower level of interest at the start, to then increase the repayments over

the first, say, five or six years and then to make level payments for the remainder of the term.

In these ways, the precise mortgage repayment terms can be adapted to suit you.

Low-start mortgages often go hand-in-hand with mortgages based on a high multiple of income. In this case, the lender is more relaxed about establishing the total loan on a higher income because the repayments will be based on a lower level of interest. Total repayments start at a lower level but can then increase later on as your income increases. However, the low-start mortgage is not necessarily a good deal for the first-time homebuyer because it is not unusual for the total loan to be restricted to, say 85% of the maximum loan. For the first-time homebuyer, this could mean having to find a cash deposit of 15% of the value of the house, which could be just as big a problem for him as finding a mortgage in the first place.

Some options for first-time buyers

As a first time buyer, you are in a privileged position because mortgage lenders are all keen to attract new business and developers offer special deals on new homes. It used to be the case that you got your mortgage from the building society you had been saving with for years, but the increased competition amongst financial institutions has created a greater choice for the buyer. Although it is by no means certain that mortgage queues won't return, for the present it is not necessary for you to show loyalty to a particular lender in order to get a mortgage loan.

Because it's often difficult for first-time buyers to qualify for loans large enough to buy houses outright, some building societies have been giving consideration to a scheme that involves them becoming joint owners with the people they are lending money to.

The scheme allows people to purchase property by reducing the repayments they have to make on their mortgages. Certain societies have decided to allow buyers to borrow up to 100% of the valuation of the property whilst paying interest on only 70% of the mortgage at current interest rates. Interest on the remainder of the loan will be at a much lower interest rate (and in some cases nothing at all) with the building society in return entitled to 30% of the increased capital value of the property when it is sold. This effectively means that whereas to qualify for a £60,000 loan the borrower would normally need an annual income of £20,000 (on a multiple of three), under this proposed scheme, he would only need an income of £14,000 as he would in effect be borrowing only 70% of the total ie £42,000.

Joint ownership

There are other avenues open to the first-time buyer and particularly those on low incomes. Faced with the seemingly impossible task of buying a house of their own, many people are now clubbing together to buy houses on a joint ownership basis.

However, this should not simply be looked at as an easy way round a financial problem. If you buy your house in this way, you now share the legal ownership of an expensive asset which will require maintenance and which will incur costs. Some of these costs will be of an easily divisible nature eg rates; others will depend on usage which may be impossible to divide up on an equitable basis eg electricity. It is important that you sort out all of these apparently trivial items right at the start.

According to the First Time Buyers Advisory Service it is a good idea to have a single contract drawn up between the buyers so that all parties are in agreement about their obligations. Typical clauses in this agreement (which should be prepared by a solicitor) should cover:

1 How should the property be held? Should it be a joint tenancy (where the property is owned jointly and where ownership passes automatically to the survivor in the event of death) or should it be tenants in common (usually used where two people of the same sex buy)?
2 In what proportions the property is held (which will usually depend on the proportions paid towards the purchase of the property)?
3 In what shares will the running costs be paid?
4 How are you going to agree on the need for maintenance and how will you sort out the payment?
5 How much notice is required if one party is forced to sell eg because of a change of job?
6 Should you build in a minimum length of time before the house can be sold for non-urgent reasons?
7 If one party wishes to sell and the other wishes to buy, what basis should you use for calculating a fair price and how should you divide up the costs incurred?
8 What happens if one of the partners dies?

The point to be made is that this agreement addresses the problems which might arise in practice (and some of them certainly *will* arise in practice). If you can't agree about these with your proposed joint owner, then perhaps you should be looking for another joint owner.

Shared ownership

Another route is shared ownership, usually of council or housing association property, where you buy a portion of the property and pay rent on the remainder, buying up the rest as you can afford it. Housing associations have traditionally provided houses and flats to rent for people on low incomes, but since the Housing Act 1980, they have been able to build and improve properties to sell. Since 1980, over

30,000 homes have been provided for sale to low income families and the elderly.

A typical scheme has been established in Gloucestershire between the District Council and a local builder. Under the scheme, tenants buy half their house and pay rent on the other half. Even taking a full mortgage on the purchased half still means monthly outgoings of less than £200. This was made possible because the Council was in the position to make grants to this kind of scheme making the full market price of the property lower than normal.

Anybody wishing to move out of this kind of housing simply contacts the local housing society to be kept on a waiting list. A purchaser is found and the couple moving out receive the original purchase money plus any extra that has been due to any increase in the value of their part of the property.

Starter homes

The homeloans scheme is a Government subsidy for those who have been saving with a registered bank or building society for more than two years. This provides you with £110 tax-free and an interest-free loan of £600 repayable in five years. Details are available from the Department of the Environment or your local Citizens Advice Bureau.

A further development for the first-time buyer has been the introduction of packages by builders that include a discount on legal fees and insurance, 'free' fixtures and fittings and 'preferential' mortgage terms. It is important to put all of this into perspective on the basis that nothing in business is free.

You should still look around for your own legal advisor, your own insurance deals and your own mortgage terms. You may find that you are able to do better on your own which means that the discounts that you're being offered are merely discounts on expensive deals in the first place. Secondly, you may well find that the price of the property is rather higher than might normally be the case in order to take account of the 'free' fixtures and fittings. As a result, if you do decide to sell within a couple of years you may find that the property is worth no more than the price you originally paid for it. The premium that you pay for your 'free' fixtures and fittings has of course disappeared because no potential buyer is going to pay the price that you paid for what is now second-hand equipment.

This kind of starter home *can* be helpful to you if you are looking for your first house but do tread carefully and make sure you're not paying over the top for the incentives.

Council houses

You may be currently living in a council house and paying rent to a local authority. In this case you have a right to buy your council house from the local authority, provided you have lived there for at least two years and have paid your rent regularly. You will also be entitled under a Government scheme to purchase your council house at a discount on the market value depending upon the number of years you have been a council tenant. This discount starts at one-third of the market value and rises to 60% if you have been a tenant for more than 30 years.

Obviously, if you buy your council house you will then become responsible for repairs and maintenance and will have to pay the rates and water rates on the property.

The council will accept joint buyers so you could buy the property jointly with one or more of your grown-up children. The council also run a sort of reservation scheme where you can ask for the purchase price to be 'frozen' and you then have up to two years to decide if you wish to go ahead.

Building societies are happy to grant mortgages for buying council houses, but you need to start the process by writing to your landlord, the council.

Life assurance and pensions

The free flow of mortgage funds has a number of spin-off effects, including an increase in the number of repossessions because people are being lent more than they can afford to repay. But above all, greater choice means you have the chance to pick the mortgage scheme that best suits your needs. House or flat buying usually coincides with a new phase in your life, one that involves a rethink of your financial arrangements. You may be newly married or simply living together as an unmarried couple. You may have started a new job that has given you a substantial increase in pay. Whatever the circumstances, getting a mortgage offers you the chance to make provision for your family with life assurance and for yourself with a pension. Chapter 6 looks more closely at these financial arrangements.

Mortgage repayments

A straightforward repayment loan is likely to be cheaper initially, but low cost endowment mortgages work out cheaper when interest rates are low (under 10%). With an endowment, you pay back the interest on a monthly basis while the endowment life assurance policy repays the capital when it matures. In fact it should return enough to give you a bit of extra cash at the end. An alternative is the so-called 'low-start' endowment which is designed so that premiums in the early years start at a low level and then gradually build up over four or five years before levelling out. These are of particular interest to the first-time home buyer because they can ease the strain of mortgage repayments in the early years when perhaps cash resources are being strained rather more than usual. Finally, there is the pension-related mortgage, the most tax efficient mortgage scheme but also, perhaps, the least flexible. A detailed look at your mortgage options is contained in Chapter 2 with the tax implications explained in Chapter 3.

Your mortgage repayments will take up a large chunk of your salary. If you have no idea how much, let's assume, for example, that you are currently taking home £1,000 a month (£12,000 a year) and that you are considering taking on a mortgage of £30,000. The monthly repayments will work out somewhere in the region of £233 after tax relief. The exact figure will depend on the type of mortgage scheme and the prevailing level of interest rates.

If you have been paying this much in rent, the mortgage payments won't come as much of a shock. But if you've been living with your family or renting in some cheaper part of the country you may have to tighten your belt considerably to deal with this outlay. If you do find it impossible to meet the repayments, tell your bank or building society as soon as you can and they will try to help you out. The worst thing you can do is pretend nothing is wrong.

The costs tend to mount up, but if you budget properly, you should be able to take them all in your stride. Among other things, you will also have to budget for insurance to cover the property and its contents. That will cost a few hundred pounds in all probability. Your lender may offer you an insurance package, but although this may be convenient, it might work out cheaper from another source. Check with some insurance companies (or see a broker) to make sure you are not being offered a more expensive policy than is necessary.

Dealing with people

From the time you arrange to view a property to the time you complete the purchase you will be dealing with a variety of professions and you will have to pull all the strands together.

If you haven't been saving with a building society or a bank and you are not sure who to approach for a mortgage, you have a number of choices. You can ask an estate agent or your usual financial adviser to recommend a lender. You can look in the Yellow Pages for a mortgage broker in your area, or better still, ask friends who have bought for a recommendation. Or you can pluck up the courage to walk into your nearest building society and ask to speak to the manager.

Choose a solicitor who has experience of domestic conveyancing. Ask your relatives or close friends if they can recommend someone who knows the area you are buying in. A good firm of solicitors should have no problems conveyancing for a property out of their area, but the local solicitor may have contacts that could speed up the process.

Keeping in touch

To ensure the buying process is as smooth and quick as possible, you should attempt to maintain good relations with all the people involved, including the seller, his solicitor, and the lender. Although it may be difficult at times, try to be as diplomatic as possible. If, for example, the seller's solicitor seems to be dragging his feet, have a tactful word with the seller, along the lines of, 'Our solicitor hasn't heard anything from your solicitor, we were wondering whether there are any problems that you are aware of'. It may be that the seller doesn't realise there is a problem. In this respect, it is good to have a solicitor who you feel you can talk to at any time and who will tell you if there is any hold-up. It is, of course, going to help you if you have a good understanding of the legal process because the whole essence of buying property is the *legal* transfer of ownership from the seller to the buyer. Chapter 5 covers this process in more detail.

Moving in

Once the buying process is completed, you will have to organise a removal van to transfer all your belongings and any furniture you may have to your new address. The cost of this operation will obviously depend on how much and how far you have to move. If you can drive and you don't have too much to move, you could hire a transit van for a day and that probably wouldn't cost you more than £50. But if you've got a whole house full of things to be moved, your best bet is to pay a removal firm to do it for you. For the contents of a three-bedroom house moving over 100 miles, the cost will be in the region of £300. The same house moving only 20 miles would be nearer £200. A two-bedroom flat moving 20 miles would probably cost around £150.

Once you are safely installed in your new home, it's unlikely that you'll have much spare cash for the bills that need to be met straightaway. One very effective way of avoiding all those lump sum payments is to open a standing order account for all your regular outgoings. Gas, electricity, domestic rates, telephone services, house and car insurance can all be paid off in monthly instalments, which will even out the financial burden.

Overall, there really does seem to be an awful lot to bear in mind when looking for and buying a home. However, you are not alone because millions of people have been through the same or similar experiences. *Buying Your Home* will help you as it deals clearly with each stage of the house buying process, explaining the options available to you and the merits of each one.

2 Your mortgage options

Whether or not you approve of political slogans, there is little denying that Britain *is* a home owning democracy. Successive governments have encouraged people to make their own way in the housing market and, whilst there may be disagreement on the extent to which we should have a mixed housing economy, the benefits of home ownership continue to be promoted.

One of the key incentives to house purchase is to give tax relief on the interest paid on money borrowed to buy a home. This has been a feature of domestic life in the United Kingdom for many years and seems set to continue for the foreseeable future regardless of which political party is in power. This aspect is covered in more detail in Chapter 6 but essentially the interest on the first £30,000 of your mortgage qualifies for tax relief at the basic and higher rate. This system of tax relief on mortgage interest was consolidated in 1983 with the introduction of MIRAS (Mortgage Interest Relief At Source). This means that interest payments on most mortgages are actually paid net of basic rate tax (with higher rate tax relief being giving through your notice of coding or year-end return).

Getting a mortgage means that you have to start thinking seriously about personal finance in order to understand fully what it is you are getting involved with. Obtaining a mortgage in these days of easy credit is not at all difficult. It is not even necessary to find a specific property to buy before applying for a mortgage. Many lenders will provide mortgage certificates which is, in effect, a promise of a mortgage when you finally find your home.

Because of this apparent simplicity, many people simply choose to switch off at this stage which means that they invariably do not get the best deal for themselves. This is particularly true when it comes to the type of mortgage they have. The lazy homebuyer probably thinks that one mortgage scheme is pretty much the same as the next one. This is not so and there are in fact three distinct types of mortgage.

Repayment mortgage

Under a repayment mortgage, monthly payments consisting of both capital and interest are made to the lender. In the early years, interest represents the larger part of each monthly repayment. Then, as more and more capital is repaid, the balance changes until, towards the end of the term of the mortgage, capital represents the larger proportion. The payments are structured so that the full amount you have borrowed is repaid by the end of the term of the mortgage (which is typically 25 years).

Under the MIRAS system, the repayments are a combination of net interest (net of basic rate tax relief) and capital. The whole system is structured so that all the repayments are the same (unless, of course, there is a change of interest rates or tax rates). There is a variation of this (often used by the banks) called the 'gross profile'. Under this system, the combined payments of *gross* interest and capital are structured so as to be level. However, as with all repayment mortgages, the proportion of each payment representing the repayment of capital steadily increases. Consequently, the *net* payment after tax relief (ie the money you actually pay out) slowly increases as well under the gross profile system (as the amount of interest on which you get tax relief slowly decreases).

The principal attraction of repayment mortgages is that they are relatively inexpensive in the early years which is often

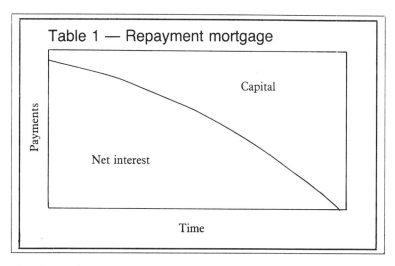

Table 1 — Repayment mortgage

the time when most house buyers are feeling the greatest cash strain. However, they do have the disadvantage that you are slowly but surely repaying the capital ie you are slowly but surely giving up a tax efficient method of borrowing money and it could just be that there are better uses to which you could put that capital.

Along with the repayment scheme, the lender will require that you take out a mortgage protection insurance policy to cover the mortgage repayments if you should die. Because mortgage protection is a form of term insurance, these policies are not expensive.

Endowment mortgage

The mechanics of an endowment mortgage are that you take out an interest-only loan for, say, 25 years with your lender. At the same time, you take out an endowment life assurance policy which will repay the mortgage when the policy matures, also in 25 years time. At the end of the policy term you may find that the maturity value is more than enough to pay off the mortgage and you may have a cash sum left over. The extra amount you receive depends upon several factors including how much the life company has made on its investments.

With a repayment mortgage, the interest element decreases over the term because you are steadily repaying the capital. However, with an endowment mortgage, you pay interest on the full amount of the mortgage during the mortgage term. Tax relief is usually available on the interest payments according to your rate of income tax so your tax relief is maximised throughout the mortgage period. Meanwhile, you are saving towards paying off the capital with your endowment policy premiums which have the added advantage that they also provide the life assurance protection needed to cover the mortgage repayment if you should die.

A variation on the endowment mortgage is the 'low cost' variety which combines an endowment policy for maybe half

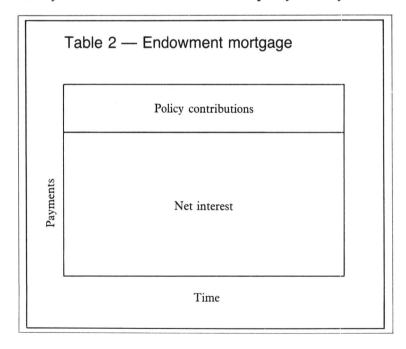

Table 2 — Endowment mortgage

Policy contributions

Net interest

Payments

Time

the capital value of the mortgage with an element of term insurance. The cost of this approach can often be lower in the first year than a repayment mortgage.

The endowment is traditionally a 'with-profits' policy, but it could be a 'unit-linked' one. It is important that you know the difference between with-profits and unit-linked because some insurance companies offer one type, and some the other.

With-profits policies

Your premium for a with-profits endowment goes partly towards your life assurance but mainly it is invested by the company in a mixture of property, shares and fixed interest securities. The investment mix is fairly conservative to reduce the risk of the value of the company's investments falling below the value guaranteed under your policy. But the end result is, of course, variable, especially as insurance

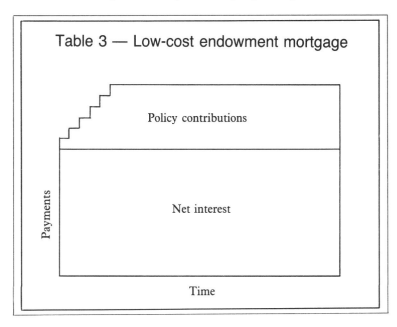

Table 3 — Low-cost endowment mortgage

Policy contributions

Net interest

Payments

Time

companies take such a long term view. Your endowment policy grows by a system of bonuses, paid out according to how much the insurance company has managed to swell its reserves and how much it decides to distribute to its with-profits policy holders. At the very end of the policy term, you may benefit further from what is known as a terminal bonus. This is not a guaranteed bonus as it usually depends upon how well the insurance company's investments have done, but if all goes well it could be a substantial sum.

When calculating the size of policy needed to pay off your mortgage, the insurance company will assume that only 80% of the current bonus scales will apply throughout the mortgage. This safety margin is used because it is not guaranteed that the present level of bonuses will be maintained. They may rise, but they may also fall. They are paid at the insurance company's discretion.

Unit-linked policies

A unit-linked policy does not work on a bonus system but is driven more directly by investment performance. These policies have become very popular over the last 20 years because they offer the chance of a better than average return based on active investment management. There are risks attached to this philosophy of course because investments don't always go up. But over the long term, which is what a life policy is designed for, unit-linked policies have proved to be a very effective alternative to the traditional form of life assurance policy. The performance of a good unit-linked policy compares very favourably with the returns available from the best with-profits policies.

Both with-profit and unit-linked endowments are now available in low-start form whereby in the first year the premium is usually around 40% cheaper than normal, but goes up over four or five years to double its original level. For the first time buyer, low-start endowments can be the cheapest type of mortgage in the all important first year of the mortgage.

Before you commit yourself to one company's products, you can check their performance against other companies in specialist periodicals such as *Money Management* and *Planned Savings*. These carry details of how each investment fund has performed, how much money is invested in the fund and what its charges are. Because of the long-term nature of the investment, it doesn't necessarily have to be the best over the last year or so, as long as the company can prove that it has a good, consistent, long-term performance record. If you find that the company has consistently not performed very well, choose one that has.

Pension-related mortgage

A pension is, in simple terms, a system of deferred pay. By giving up some of your income now and paying it into a pension plan, you build up a fund which will provide you with an income when you retire.

The benefits of a pension plan can be taken in two ways:

(a)   you can take a lifetime income (ie one that is paid for the rest of your life); or
(b)   you can take part of the fund as a tax-free cash lump sum and take the balance as a smaller lifetime income.

It is this second method of taking benefits that provides the basis of a pension-related mortgage and its attraction is due in no small way to the fact that all contributions to a pension plan are tax-free.

The workings of a pension-related mortgage are similar to an endowment. You pay interest over the term of the mortgage and this will be paid net of basic rate tax under the MIRAS system. When you come to retirement age, you will be allowed to take part of your pension fund as a tax-free cash lump sum and it is out of this lump sum that you pay off your mortgage. The remainder of the fund is then used to provide you with an income for your retirement.

The advantages of a pension-related mortgage over an endowment mortgage are based on the fact that not only do you get tax relief on the mortgage interest payments but also on the contributions that you make to the pension plan. In addition, the insurance company does not have to pay any tax on the income or capital gains earned within the pension fund (as it does with an endowment policy which is linked to a life assurance fund). This means that the retirement fund that is being built up with your contributions has the potential to grow at a faster rate than other tax bearing investments.

The advantage of this type of mortgage over a repayment mortgage is obvious. Instead of repaying capital to the building society, you are investing it into a pension plan with these twin tax benefits. It therefore represents a very tax efficient way of repaying your mortgage.

There are a whole series of different rules concerning the type of pension plan you may take out, the level of contributions you may make to it and the benefits that you can take from the various types of pension scheme. A detailed discussion of these is beyond the scope of this book but it would be a sensible move to get professional guidance in this area to find out if you can take advantage of a pension-related mortgage.

Pension mortgages may involve a greater monthly outlay than a comparable repayment or endowment mortgage and can be for a longer period. But because of the tax relief the ultimate return is significantly greater than you would get from either of the alternatives. You can see from the examples in this chapter that the initial gross pension mortgage is much more than you end up paying. The end result will often justify the greater initial outlay.

One important point to bear in mind in a pension-related mortgage is, of course, that you are repaying the loan out of your pension benefits ie your pension benefits at retirement are going to be reduced. Consequently, although taking out a pension mortgage is a very tax efficient way of repaying your loan, you should consider making alternative arrangements as you get older in order that your pension benefits can remain untouched. As the demands on your income get less, it may be well worth your while taking out an additional *endowment* plan in order to repay the loan and to preserve the full value of your pension.

Using your company pension scheme

Members of company pension schemes may also be able to take advantage of a similar facility which allows for the loan to be repaid from the tax-free cash available from the scheme. The amount of cash available is calculated differently, being based on your length of service with your employer and your salary at retirement. The statement of the benefits available to you under the scheme, which you should be able to obtain from the trustees, together with the member's handbook, will normally give the lender details of the anticipated cash sum available.

Once again, it is worth remembering that pension benefits are being given up to repay the mortgage and it is therefore worth considering Additional Voluntary Contributions (AVCs) as a means of repaying the income which you will be giving up in order to repay the mortgage. In keeping with other forms of pension contributions, AVCs benefit from full tax relief and are therefore a highly efficient means of saving.

Lifetime loans

As an alternative (and this applies to both endowment mortgages and pension mortgages), a recent development has been the concept of the 'lifetime loan' option. This incorporates the facility to borrow on an interest-only basis but provides for the capital to be repaid out of the borrower's estate when he dies. Under these circumstances, you won't have to repay the capital at the end of any particular period but will exercise an option to continue the loan until you die. There is therefore no need to use up *any* tax-free cash emerging from your pension scheme to repay the loan (but there is, of course, the need to ensure that there is sufficient income in retirement to enable you to continue the interest payments and life assurance premiums). Consequently, there's still good sense in increasing your pension contributions to build up the maximum pension you can obtain and at the same time you take out a suitable whole life assurance policy, assigned to the lender, which will pay off the loan on your death.

Personal pensions

The personal pensions market has been given an enormous boost by the Government's recent far-reaching pension reforms. The major aim of the legislation is greater freedom for individuals to choose their own pension scheme. Individuals will have the chance to find the scheme which best suits their needs, for example, employees will be able to opt out of their occupational scheme or the State Earnings Related Pension Scheme (SERPS) in order to invest in a private pension arrangement. These new personal pensions (which will also be the way in which the self-employed and employees who are not in an occupational scheme can provide for their retirement benefits) may also be used as a means of repaying a mortgage.

Comparison

Generally speaking, the lower the interest rate, the more attractive endowment and pension mortgages become. However, because taking out a pension mortgage is a relatively complex matter involving more than just repaying a mortgage, you should take advice from a professional financial adviser, your mortgage broker, your accountant or even your solicitor. For all its tax efficiency, the pension mortgage can seem slightly unwieldy and inflexible at times.

The following tables compare the likely costs of each of the three types of mortgage. It is important not to pay too much attention to the exact figures as these are intended only as a guide, and of course over a 25-year period interest rates and tax rates are likely to vary and affect the monthly payments you will need to make.

The important point is to understand the concept of the three approaches and to decide which is most likely to suit your particular circumstances or which you feel will be the best value for you. Whichever approach you take, the most important point is to ensure that you can afford the repayments.

Variations

As with most things in life, there are always variations on a theme and mortgages are no exception. As competition increases in the world of lending, new (and some not so new) terms or descriptions of facilities will be seen.

Here are some of the newer terms you might come across in your trawl of the mortgage market these days:

Mortgage rate The rate charged by that particular lender. Not usually directly connected to any other rate so try to find out the lender's past track record and not just their current rate.

LIBOR (London Inter Bank Offered Rate) The rate at which the major UK banks lend each other money. Some lenders offer schemes at a fixed percentage over LIBOR. LIBOR

Table 4: The three types of mortgage – how they compare

£30,000 MIRAS mortgage loan for 25 years at 10% interest. Self-employed male, non-smoker aged 39, earning £20,000 pa (basic rate taxpayer).

	Repayment £	Endowment £	Pension £
Capital repayment	37.86	–	–
Interest at 10%	250.00	250.00	250.00
Tax relief at 25%	62.50	62.50	62.50
Net monthly payment	225.36	187.50	187.50
Premiums/contributions	14.34[1]	45.21[2]	69.95[3]
Tax relief at 25%	–	–	17.48
Net monthly premiums	14.34	45.21	52.47
Total net monthly cost	£239.70	£232.71	£239.97
Residual value at end of 25 years	None[4]	Some cash[5]	Cash or pension[6]

Notes
1 Convertible term assurance rates
2 Assuming 7.5% pa net fund growth
3 Based on retirement age 65, life cover built in and assuming 12% pa net fund growth
4 Repayment mortgages are aimed to repay exactly the loan amount so there will be no money left over.

£30,000 MIRAS mortgage loan for 25 years at 12.5% interest. Self-employed male, non-smoker, aged 39, earning £20,000 pa (basic rate taxpayer).

	Repayment £	*Endowment* £	*Pension* £
Capital repayment	28.98		
Interest at 12½%	312.50	312.50	312.50
Tax relief at 25%	78.13	78.13	78.13
Net monthly payment	263.35	234.37	234.37
Premiums/contributions	14.34[1]	45.21[2]	69.95[3]
Tax relief at 25%	–	–	17.48
Net monthly premiums	14.34	45.21	52.47
Total net monthly cost	£277.69	£279.58	£286.84
Residual value at end of 25 years	None[4]	Some cash[5]	Cash or pension[6]

5 Quite often the performance of the endowment plan policy will be a little better than originally expected and so there will be a maturity value. In some cases you may be able to pay off the loan a year or so early instead of taking the cash.
6 The pension fund growth rate may be better than expected and could therefore increase the lump sum taken at retirement or the cash could be used to increase your pension income.

itself tends to be more volatile than other interest rates so you *could* end up making substantial savings, but this option is definitely not for the cautious.

Fixed interest Most mortgages are variable rate ie the rate changes from time to time. Fixed interest schemes set the rate at outset usually for three to five years. They can be attractive if interest rates go up, but are bad news if they go down and getting out could involve paying an early redemption penalty.

Early redemption penalty A charge for not running your mortgage to its full term. Acceptable if the rate is low and especially if the charge falls away after one or two years but could be expensive when you move house or mortgage.

Low start or flexible mortgage You choose to pay less than the interest *charged*. Your outstanding mortgage consequently goes up but the lower initial costs can make it a good deal in the early years. Interest rates charged can however be higher – you pay for the flexibility.

Stabilised payment schemes Often applies where payments are set once a year but interest *charged* can change in the meanwhile. Can be useful to help your budgeting.

Secured credit line (or agreed drawdown facility) The lender decides how much they are prepared to lend you and you take what you want now with the balance being available over usually the first five years of your mortgage easily and quickly. Useful for things like school fees planning.

Drop lock Sounds like a rugby term but is actually an option for people with variable payment mortgages to 'drop' into a fixed ('lock') interest rate scheme. Who invents these terms anyway?

Cap and collar A maximum (and in the case of a collar, a minimum) rate of interest which you could be charged during the period the cap or collar applies, regardless of the lender's normal interest rate at the time. An extra one-off charge is usually made for caps.

Securitisation The selling of a group of loans by your lender to someone else. Usually your lender retains full administrative control and still sets interest rates etc, so in practice it will have little effect on your particular mortgage.

There is no limit to man's ingenuity in devising a new selling angle to a familiar subject – mortgages. If you are sufficiently interested in the more esoteric regions of the mortgage market, you should certainly seek professional advice during your quest.

Bridging loans

As well as a long-term mortgage loan to pay for your new house, you may need a short-term loan to bridge the gap between buying and selling houses. This will be a useful but expensive option when you need money quickly to buy a house, but your own money is still tied up in your previous property. If you anticipate some delay in selling your current house, contact your bank and as long as you can satisfy them that the house will be sold eventually, they should grant you the loan.

One helpful point is that tax relief (see Chapter 3) can be claimed on interest paid on bridging loans up to £30,000, but only for one year. During this period any tax relief claimed can be in addition to any relief claimed on a main mortgage loan.

The thing to bear in mind about bridging loans is that they are meant as short-term, stop-gap loans. Bank managers don't encourage open-ended bridging loans, and will probably charge you a £150 arrangement fee for such a privilege. Arrangement fees under normal circumstances where you are simply bridging the deposit on a mortgage, will be in the region of £75. The interest rate in all cases will be in the region of 4% over the bank base rates, so it could be a costly exercise if you keep the loan on for any length of time. In any event, you should not keep a bridging loan going for more than a few months, certainly not more than a year.

Increasing your mortgage and re-mortgages

Once you have moved into your new home, you may at some time decide to do some major alterations to it, for example, you may decide to install a central heating system or perhaps build an extension. Whatever the venture, you probably won't have the money for it so it's time to go back to your friendly lender. This should be your first port of call. Tell them what you want to do and ask if you can have this extra money added to your mortgage loan. As long as the scheme isn't too expensive (and provided the value of your property will adequately cover the existing loan and the extra loan) the lender should be only too happy to grant you the extra cash, especially if it is going towards adding value to the property. If not, then try another lender. You may be offered the option of extending the mortgage term as well, which could mean that your monthly repayments remain pretty much as they are.

Despite the abolition of tax relief on loans for home improvements in the 1988 Budget, this form of extended credit remains one of the best there is. Not only are you borrowing at a competitive rate of interest but if the loan itself is stretched over a long period you will hardly notice the difference from your original mortgage.

The increased competition in lending generally means that you can now often get a further advance on your mortgage for virtually anything, even things totally unrelated to your property.

However, a word of warning. If your new loan is still within the £30,000 limit and may therefore qualify for tax relief, it does not pay to be 'economical with the truth'. The Inland Revenue take an extremely dim view of anybody claiming tax relief on a top-up loan which is being used for something other than buying their home and are quite prepared to prosecute people who have made false claims for mortgage interest relief.

Beware of lenders who will only advance you the money as a personal loan rather than as a further advance. Personal loans tend to be more expensive and are often only available over shorter terms, making the monthly outlay very high relative to the amount borrowed.

Re-mortgaging is an alternative for those wishing to raise cash, but who can't do so from their original lending source. All you are basically doing is transferring your mortgage to another lender. This is not a course of action you should jump at without finding out what it will cost. You may be penalised by the original lender, or charged a higher rate of interest by the new one and will in any event have fresh legal and valuation fees to pay. Enlist the assistance and advice of a financial expert.

Now that you have your mortgage sorted out, it's worth exploring further the tax implications of buying and owning a home. The next chapter explains more.

Useful contacts

Money Management (Financial Times Business Information) – Tel: 01–405 6969
Planned Savings (United Trade Press) – Tel: 01–837 1212

3 Tax aspects of house buying

Considering all the other incidental expense involved, the surprising thing about buying your own home is how little tax you pay. In fact, in the right circumstances, the tax man ends up giving you hundreds of pounds.

The taxes which are involved

There are three main personal taxes that affect the home owner.

Income tax Most home buyers will get tax relief on at least part of the interest payments that they make on their mortgage. This is a valuable benefit to the home owner and, as most of us are basic rate taxpayers the MIRAS system deals fully with the available relief for the majority of borrowers.

Capital gains tax A property is a capital asset and so it is *potentially* the subject of capital gains tax when you sell it. However, for most home buyers, this is not a tax to worry about because there is a specific relief for any gain made on your home.

Inheritance tax Inheritance tax is another form of capital taxation which occurs when we give things away either voluntarily (when we are alive) or involuntarily (when we die). This is a tax which will affect significant numbers of people – including many people who don't necessarily consider themselves to be wealthy. For the home buyer, it's a time to consider the implications of your new financial situation and to consider re-writing your will in order to reduce the impact of this tax.

Income tax and MIRAS

The principal tax concession for buyers is the relief granted on interest payments on up to £30,000 of mortgage borrowings. If the loan you are getting is to buy the property you are going to live in, you are eligible for this relief. The basic rate (currently 25%) tax-payer will pay 75p of each £1 of interest on the first £30,000 of his loan and tax relief covers the rest. Higher rate (currently 40%) tax payers get tax relief at their top rate and the Exchequer ends up paying even more.

From 1 August 1988, there will no longer be any advantage to 'living in sin' for the purposes of obtaining two lots of mortgage interest relief. Until then, of course, unmarried couples buying together can still both qualify for £30,000 worth of relief. So if you are taking out a £60,000 loan and are making equal contributions to its repayment, you get relief on the full amount of interest rather than just on the interest on the first £30,000. Where a couple are borrowing more than £30,000 but less than £60,000 and one of them is a higher rate tax payer, that person should be paying interest on a full £30,000 of the mortgage with the partner taking up the remainder. However, make sure you pay for the mortgage from a joint bank account so that it is clear that you are both paying the interest on the mortgage repayment.

The new rules on mortgage interest relief, operative from 1 August 1988, permit tax relief of £30,000 to be granted per property, regardless of how many people are buying together and whether or not they are married.

Two or more unmarried people buying together will be allocated equal shares of the £30,000 worth of relief. However, a husband and wife will be able to share the interest relief in whatever proportions they wish, irrespective of which of them is actually paying off the interest.

What qualifies for tax relief?

The rules for income tax relief on mortgage loans are quite detailed but the principal ones are as follows:

1 Any interest which you pay on a loan raised to buy land or buildings in the UK is potentially eligible for tax relief. The interest on any loan that you raise to pay off another qualifying loan is also eligible.
2 The type of loan included in the rules covers bank loans, building society mortgages and so on. It does *not* include overdraft interest.
3 When you pay the interest, you must be the current owner of the property (although a couple living together would usually get tax relief if, for example, the husband buys a property and the wife pays the interest).

Home improvement loans no longer qualify for mortgage interest relief. Tax relief on loans for the purchase or improvement of a residence for a spouse or dependent relative has also been abolished, as of 6 April 1988. The equivalent capital gains tax relief on homes provided for dependent relatives is also abolished for disposals on or after 6 April 1988.

How is tax relief obtained?

Basic rate tax is deducted at source when making interest payments to most lenders. This means that your monthly repayment is calculated *net* of basic rate tax relief. Those buyers who have received funding from a lender not covered by the MIRAS scheme have to pay their mortgage interest gross and claim the tax relief back from the Inland Revenue by way of obtaining an increased tax code.

If you are a higher rate taxpayer, then you continue to pay your interest payments net of basic rate tax only and recover any higher rate tax repayment direct from the Inland Revenue through your notice of coding.

The current rules on tax relief on mortgage interest may not be with us forever. The threshold was raised from £25,000 to £30,000 in 1983 and while there is a chance that a future Government may increase it again to better reflect the rise in prices, it is equally likely that a future Government may cut back the level of relief to basic rate only or (less likely) abolish it altogether.

In Chapter 2 the comparative cost of a £30,000 mortgage at 12.5% for a basic rate tax payer was shown to be around £280 a month (net). However, an unmarried couple, who are both higher rate tax payers (40%) could get a £60,000 endowment mortgage for a total net monthly outlay of only £471 due to the higher rate tax relief on two £30,000 loans. However, the Chancellor has fixed a final date for these schemes: 1 August 1988.

Profits from a home based business are treated as revenue transactions for the purposes of tax assessment and therefore subject to income tax at your highest marginal rate. For further information on taxation of businesses, consult the latest *Allied Dunbar Tax Guide*.

Capital gains tax

Your home is a capital asset and so in theory is likely to be subject to capital gains tax. Capital gains tax (CGT) is exactly what it says – a tax on a capital gain ie the difference between the buying price and the selling price of an asset.

There are, however, special rules and exemptions on CGT and one of these specifically relates to private residences and, in particular, your *main* residence. When you buy your home, you should tell your local inspector of your purchase by completing the appropriate section of your annual income tax return (the section which asks for details of 'chargeable assets acquired').

The main exemption that you have as a home buyer is that provided the property you buy and sell is your main residence, you will not have any liability to CGT when you sell it.

If you own a second home, then CGT may affect you and you'll find more details in Chapter 8.

There may be a CGT charge on your main residence if you have let part of it out. According to the Department of the Environment leaflet, *Letting Rooms in Your Home*, when the resident landlord comes to sell, that part of the house which is not let will continue to be exempt from CGT under the normal rules. The part that has been let to tenants will also be exempt for capital gains tax provided:

(a) it is not self contained;
(b) the gain is not more than £20,000 during the time it has been let;
(c) the gain is not more than the gain made on the part which is not let.

If you are in any doubt about your tax position seek professional advice. For more on tax and your home as a business, consult Chapter 9.

The key point to remember here is always to keep the Inland Revenue informed when you buy or sell property. They always like to know these things and it's always helpful if you give them confirmation of what your solicitor is obliged to tell them by law anyway.

Inheritance tax

This is the one tax which many people forget all about because they don't regard themselves as wealthy, but it affects far more people than is popularly imagined. In very simple terms, if you die and own assets worth more than £110,000 then the excess is taxed at 40%. The threshold is index-linked but it is still most important to keep a close eye on the potential impact of inheritance tax on your estate given the dramatic rise in house prices in recent years.

Fortunately, there are a number of exemptions to inheritance tax and one of those is particularly relevant to married couples. If you die and leave your possessions to your husband or wife, then there is no inheritance tax liability. If, however, you leave possessions to your family (which is bound to be the case when the *second* of you dies) then inheritance tax *is* potentially payable and can mean that your children are saddled with a very heavy tax bill indeed.

Don't forget that inheritance tax isn't just levied on the value of your home. It is applied to the total value of everything you own when you die – house, car, house contents, cash in the bank, value of life assurance policies – everything. It would therefore not be at all unusual to find that having left the family home in your will to your family, they then have to sell it in order to pay the tax on it.

Inheritance tax planning can be very straightforward and there are some very simple ways in which this potential tax bill can be met so that your family is protected. The most straightforward way is to make it part of your regular financial planning and to take out a suitably arranged life assurance policy which will pay the tax for you. Your usual financial adviser will be able to give you all the details.

Having made sure that your mortgage and tax position are now on a sound footing, it is time to look at the actual buying process, the paperwork involved and the people you will meet.

4 Estate agents, valuations and surveys

Of all the people with whom you will deal in the house buying process, the estate agent is the one most people love to hate. As an intermediary, gamely matching buyer and seller, the estate agent has to learn to walk a narrow tightrope. House buying and selling is one of the most stressful times of life, and it is the estate agent who often suffers the backlash (although there are plenty of frustrated buyers and sellers who feel that some estate agents are responsible for much of the stress in the first place).

The estate agent's role

The important point to bear in mind is that although, as a buyer, you may approach a number of estate agents to enlist their help, their first loyalty is to the *seller*. That's where the estate agent derives most of his income ie the commission he gets on a successful house sale.

Nevertheless, in order to do his job for the seller, he is also obliged to assist you, the buyer, as far as possible.

The estate agent's role is to furnish you with details of all the property on his books that fits your price range. When you contact a firm, they will want to know what sort of property you are looking for (house or flat? one or two bedrooms?), which area you want to live in and how much you are prepared to pay.

At this point one possible strategy is to underplay your hand. If the top price you could possibly afford is £55,000, tell the agent you would be prepared to pay £50,000. He will send you details of the more expensive properties anyway, but you don't want to give him the impression that you've got lots of money, because he will remember that when you try to negotiate a price later on.

However, you also have to be fairly cautious to make sure that this strategy doesn't backfire on you. If you are actually prepared to spend up to £55,000, it's quite possible that there might be houses on the estate agent's books for £60,000 where he might be able to bring buyer and seller together in order to negotiate a deal at a price somewhere between the two figures.

Get in touch with two or three agents who are well represented in the area. You will receive details of all suitable properties and be put on the mailing list for any others that come the agent's way.

Estate agent 'speak'

Estate agents use their own special variation of English, embellishing the facts without telling outright fibs. Here are a few examples of estate agent speak along with some helpful translation for the uninitiated:

- needs attention   = will cost thousands to put right
- cosy and airy   = small and draughty
- fair decorative order = the place is a mess
- proportions galore   = it's an odd shape
- equidistant from   = miles from anywhere
- secluded   = ditto
- unusual   = unsellable
- small garden   = for small, read tiny
- priced to sell   = make me an offer

That's all slightly tongue-in-cheek but most people have their

favourite anecdote about the estate agent's particulars that
went over the top. One particularly outlandish example which
appeared in a Sunday newspaper achieved new levels of
pretentiousness when it described an outside lavatory as a
'gardener's toilet'.

There's an important point to be made which is that the estate
agent's particulars have no real legal significance at all as far
as representing the property is concerned. If you buy your
house and rely *entirely* on the estate agent to provide you
with particulars, then you may have no legal redress if you
feel that the property has been misrepresented.

Don't be put off by an advert that says, 'needs redecoration'
or 'in need of modernisation' because such a property will
usually be priced cheaper than it would be in a modernised
state. There are bargains to be had with properties like this.

Avoiding the traps

When it comes to buying a house or flat, most people throw
caution to the wind; they tend to get emotionally attached to
a property too soon in the process. It is an easy trap to fall
into, but one you should try to avoid as far as possible.
Clearly the whole basis of buying is to find something you
like, but if the seller or his agent senses that you will buy
the property at any price, you are throwing away any
opportunity for negotiation which you might have.

To get the best value you can, you should do your homework.
Look at other properties in the area and the prices they are
fetching. That way you will know at a glance whether a
property is good value or not. This is especially true in
London and the Home Counties, where there are many sub-
standard properties selling at inflated prices purely because
of their situation.

The agent will often tell you there are other people interested
in a particular property, whether there are or not. If there are

no people following you round, then you might feel it safe to assume you can offer less than the asking price. If they are queuing up to see it, that shows you there is a demand for this type of property and you may have to offer the asking price if you are convinced it is good value.

The secret is to act as coolly and professionally as you can, especially in the initial stages, when you first see the property and in subsequent discussions with the seller or his agent. If you want to negotiate the price, remember that the estate agent wants to earn his selling commission, so it is in his interests to put your offer to the seller and to try and reach an agreement, even if this means splitting the difference.

The more properties you see, the easier it will be to assess what is good value and what isn't. So whatever you do, don't make an offer on the first place you see, you can always go back.

Valuations and surveys

Lender's valuation

Before you are granted a mortgage, the lender will want to arrange an inspection of the property. Although they may refer to this as a survey, it will probably only be a brief visit to assess the value, rather than any detailed structural analysis. Even so, you could easily find yourself paying £100 or more for this fairly cursory inspection. Because the basic valuation report is so limited, any defects in the property may go undetected, so if you have any doubts, arrange for a more detailed inspection to be carried out.

House Buyer's Report

If the property is fairly new and purpose-built, a detailed survey may not be essential. But if it is an old property or it has had some conversion work done, a structural survey should be carried out. You can usually arrange this through your lender and you can often instruct the firm who are handling the valuation for them, with some savings in costs. They may offer you a choice, dependent on whether you just want the basic valuation report described above, a brief Royal Institution of Chartered Surveyors House Buyer's Report, or the full structural survey which will also be carried out by a member of the RICS.

The second option, the House Buyer's Report, will be about five pages long and contain a general description of the property. You should expect to pay at least £150 for this, and if it's a fairly new building you can be content with that. But if it is a Victorian property, or even older than that, only a full structural survey will reveal whether the property is solid and secure.

Structural survey

The full structural survey and report should be between ten and fifteen pages long and cover the following areas:

(a) a general description of the property, including details of construction, boundaries, exact dimensions, accommodation, fixtures and fittings;

(b) an appraisal of the condition of the property, to include foundations, external and internal walls, roofing, flooring and ceilings, chimney stacks, fascia and soffit boards, pipes, drains and gutters, windows and any external joinery, doors and any communal hallways;

(c) examination of any gardens or pathways attaching to the property, especially trees that may be diseased or liable to cause subsidence;

(d)   comments on the efficiency of the utilities and services provided, ie, water, electricity, gas, telephone etc;

(e)   details of all known charges relating to the property such as ground rent, service charges and rates;

(f)   comments on any recent or pending building repairs and how this affects the buyer.

In addition to these points, you should raise any specific queries you may have with the surveyor so that he can include his assessment within the structural survey.

Independent survey

If you want your own private assessment of the state of the property, you can use an independent surveyor. That is, your own choice of surveyor rather than the lender's. Alternatively, you may opt for the lender's basic valuation (which will only give you an idea of whether the lender believes the property to be adequate security for the mortgage) and then have the property surveyed yourself independently to get an idea of its true market value.

The cost of a survey varies widely but it should not amount to more than £250 for a two bedroom flat or £350 for a three bedroom house. It is simply a case of shopping around. Make sure the surveyor has the letters ARICS or FRICS after his name to show that he is either an Associate or a Fellow of the Royal Institution of Chartered Surveyors.

It's worth making the point that many lenders are now insisting on having a valuation of the property carried out by their own panel valuer and may not be prepared to let your valuer complete their forms. This is something that is becoming more common, and is a regrettable reaction to the very high number of fraud cases that have been found in recent years.

What a good survey should tell you

A good survey should give you as much information as you need to assess how secure the property is and how much work will need to be done once you move in. Most properties have something wrong with them, but it may only be cosmetic and therefore not very costly or problematic. On the other hand, if the survey reveals that the house has dry rot or weak foundations, or it needs a new roof, you should think again about buying it.

If you feel you can afford to have the repairs made good, assuming that is possible, try to renegotiate the price with the seller or the estate agent. The danger here of course is that the seller may turn round and offer the property to someone else. This is where you need to keep calm and avoid being forced into a corner. You have to decide whether to stand your ground and risk being gazumped, or make a higher offer. The chances are that if there is something wrong with the property the seller will have problems finding another buyer, unless the alternative buyer doesn't have a proper survey done, in which case the problems may go undetected. You will probably sleep more soundly if you stand your ground.

Useful contacts

National Association of Estate Agents – Tel: 0926 496800
Royal Institution of Chartered Surveyors – Tel: 01–222 7000

5 Solicitors and the conveyancing process

What is conveyancing?

The dictionary definition of conveyancing is 'the transfer of property from one person to another by deed or writing'. This process is therefore the most important aspect of buying your home. The process of conveyancing provides you with your *legal* ownership of the property and it is most important that the process is done correctly to ensure that your legal title to your home is good.

An important point to note is that there are some significant differences in the conveyancing process in Scotland compared to the rest of the United Kingdomn. These differences are so profound that if you are selling property in England and moving to Scotland (or vice versa), then you are almost certainly going to need the help of two solicitors. The first part of this chapter will deal with the English system; a later section will explain the differences in the Scottish system.

Conveyancing in England

The English system of property conveyancing (transferring ownership from one person to another) can be complex and laborious. Fortunately, the burden of seeing the process through can be taken up by an experienced solicitor on your behalf. Some home buyers choose to do all the conveyancing

themselves, in order to save paying solicitor's fees, but the
vast majority of buyers still feel happier leaving it to someone
more experienced.

Assuming that you would like your home buying to be a
smooth and speedy process, you should attempt to have the
services of a solicitor available before you start house hunting.
It's not essential but it means you can strike while the iron
is hot. If you haven't instructed a solicitor by the time you
make your first offer, that is your top priority. Do it the
same day.

You may not have a solicitor in mind, in which case ask your
relatives and friends for recommendations. Contact two or
three firms to see what they charge for conveyancing. The
average charge is in the region of 1% of the purchase price,
but with competition increasing you should be able to find
one that charges only 0.5%. So, for example, if the price of
the property you are looking to buy is £75,000, the solicitor's
fee could be as low as £375. Don't forget to find out whether
the quoted fee includes VAT. If it doesn't, it goes up by 15%.

What the solicitor does

The system of conveyancing revolves initially around the draft
contract drawn up by the vendor's solicitor. Your solicitor's
main responsibility is to check this contract to ensure that
you are buying a legally secure property, free of any
problems. The solicitor is therefore the crucial element in the
process and it is important to choose one who you feel
confident will do a good job on your behalf.

The firm's first move will be to ascertain all the basic facts
about the sale ie the address of the property, who currently
owns it, how much you have offered for it, whether you have
a mortgage sorted out yet and how quickly you would like
to move. The more positive you can be, the more helpful and

efficient the solicitor is likely to be. If he senses that you are not serious about buying, he may not do any more than the bare minimum in terms of chasing people for information.

Your solicitor will want to make contact with the seller's solicitor as a matter of priority. If you have made an offer you should already have quite a detailed knowledge of the property, eg the length of any lease and any extras such as rates and service charges. Make a point of asking the seller for the name and address of his solicitor and pass this, together with the other information, on to yours.

Preliminary enquiries

Your solicitor may then make preliminary (pre-contract) enquiries about the property. Among other things he will enquire when the vendor is likely to be able to give vacant possession (ie when can you move in). The solicitor's standard answer to this is 'subject to contract'. No sensible solicitor will commit his client to a specific move-out date so early in the process. Similarly, any terms discussed between yourself, and the vendor, or your respective solicitors, before exchange of contracts, must be qualified with the phrase 'subject to contract'.

The preliminary enquiries form will also ask for details of any lease and what the property is currently used for. There will be questions about walls and fences, access, drainage, water, electricity and gas, fixtures and fittings, any restrictions on use, and any disputes or defects affecting the property.

At the end of the preliminary enquiries exercise, there may still be more questions than answers. Your solicitor will be able to fill in some of the gaps eg by studying any lease involved. Other answers may come from the results of the local authority search, which should be instigated as soon as possible.

Local search

The local search involves the solicitor sending a standard form to the land charges department of the local authority. The form contains questions about matters such as major development schemes for the area and how these affect the property you are buying.

The other part of a local search consists of the enquiries. These are incorporated in a standard form which is in two sections:

(a)   a list of *standard* enquiries which will cover such points as whether or not the road in which the property stands has been adopted by the local Council; and

(b)   a list of *specific* enquiries some of which may apply to the property, for example, are there any road improvements planned in the local area. This form also gives you the opportunity to make your own *personal* enquiries that only the local authority will be able to answer.

Replies to these enquiries will be given in writing by the local authority and, in most cases, it is vitally important that you wait for the answers to these questions before proceeding with the property purchase. Consequently, a local search carried out by yourself is unlikely to reveal what might be quite important aspects about the property and for this reason, most lenders will insist on waiting until the full process has been completed.

If you are really in a hurry, all is not lost. Some lenders have what is called a 'local search indemnity policy' which means that your property purchase can go ahead without waiting for the results of the local search and which will then provide indemnity *for the lender* in case anything unpleasant turns up later. However, note that the cover is for the lender, not for you.

When your solicitor receives a reply from the local authority,

he should bring any important points raised to your attention
and explain the implications. If he doesn't, make a point of
asking whether there was anything untoward about the
replies. It is important to keep the solicitor on his toes.

Restrictions

Close liaison with your solicitor does not mean you have to
badger him every day for something new, but it is probably
a good idea to meet him once or twice so that he can explain
what is happening. For instance, when the conveyancing
process is well under way, he may suggest that you meet so
that he can explain the contents of the lease to you, if you
are buying a leasehold property.

As there are probably more freeholders in the country than
there are leaseholders, the peculiar problems of buying a
lease do not apply to everybody. Some freeholds contain
restrictive covenants, but generally speaking, freeholds do
not need to be checked as thoroughly as leases.

Exchange of contracts

Once the basic terms of the sale have been agreed, contracts
can be exchanged, and the deposit paid (often 10% of the
purchase price but you may be able to negotiate a lower
percentage) at which point both parties are committed to the
deal. A completion date should also be fixed. If there is a
chain of buying and selling, it is important that the exchange
of contracts on each transaction takes place simultaneously,
to avoid a situation where you become committed to a
purchase just as your sale falls through. It's also most
important that your solicitor checks that you have a formal
mortgage offer from your lender before he exchanges contracts
on your behalf. If things go wrong at this stage, you could
find yourself with a commitment to buy a house and no
mortgage with which to buy it.

Following the exchange of contracts, correspondence continues between your solicitor, the vendor's solicitor and whoever is lending you the money. Your solicitor will make what are known as 'requisitions on title' which basically means that having checked the title deeds or the register of title he will ask further questions of the vendor's solicitor. This may be accompanied by a draft transfer form, or draft conveyance, which will ultimately operate to transfer the legal ownership of the property to you.

The lender who is granting the mortgage will also want to satisfy himself that the legal end is satisfactory and that all the paperwork is in order.

Once the contracts are exchanged and he has investigated legal title to his satisfaction, your solicitor (who will usually also be acting for your mortgage lender) will confirm to the lender that all is well and ask for the cheque for the mortgage advance.

In the meantime, the vendor's solicitor should have told the local authority about the change of ownership so that the domestic rates can be apportioned accordingly. Having worked out how much the vendor is liable for, his solicitor compiles a completion statement that specifies exactly how much is owed by you on completion, taking into account the apportionment of rates and how much deposit has already been paid.

Costs

Your solicitor will then prepare his own financial statement which, assuming there is no chain involved, will ask you to pay the balance of the vendor's completion statement, your solicitor's fees, disbursements and stamp duty at 1% of the property purchase price, less whatever mortgage you are getting.

An example is shown in Table 5. If you pay by banker's draft, the payment will go through more quickly.

Table 5: Solicitor's completion statement

Purchase of: 9 The Heath, Anytown.

		£
Purchase price of property		69,950.00
Less		
Mortgage money received	30,000	
Deposit received from you	6,995	
From sale of: 127 London Road	28,500	65,495.00
		4,455.00
Plus		
Stamp duty to Inland Revenue		699.50
Land Registry fee		165.00
Local Land Charges search fee		14.40
Central Land Charges search fee		1.00
Our account (attached)		475.00
VAT (on our account)		71.25
Balance due to us		£5,881.15

You then sign the conveyance or transfer which is sent to the vendor for signature. At the same time you will sign the mortgage deed (or legal charge as it is often called).

Completion

On completion day your solicitor will hand over the purchase price and receive the title deeds to the property in return. The keys will then be available to you and the house is yours.

This explanation of conveyancing does not include every single detail of the process. Much of this mountain of paperwork is couched in convoluted legalese and it is this as much as anything that makes conveyancing difficult for us ordinary mortals to understand and carry out. Don't even dream of doing your own conveyancing if you are easily

Table 6: Buying your home – key events flowchart

You are interested in a particular property, you tell the estate agent of your interest and arrange to view it.

You make an offer on the property and your offer is accepted (verbally).

You see your solicitor and he sends off the legal searches on the property and asks for and receives a draft contract from the vendor's solicitor.

You arrange for a mortgage via bank, building society or other financial institution. You arrange for a surveyor to survey the property.

If the draft contract is acceptable you then sign it and hand over to your solicitor a cheque for the deposit (usually 10% of the agreed purchase price).

Your solicitor and the vendor's solicitor exchange signed contracts (usually) by post.

The vendor's solicitor sends details of the legal title to the property which your solicitor examines.

Your solicitor draws up the conveyance and mortgage Deed for you to sign and sends them to the vendor's solicitor for the vendor to sign.

The lender sends the mortgage money to your solicitor. You hand over to your solicitor a cheque for the balance of the purchase price (often from the sale of your current house).

Your solicitor telegraphs the money to the vendor's solicitor and he in turn undertakes to send to your solicitor the conveyance and other deeds.

On receipt of your money the purchase is complete and the property is yours.

intimidated by officialdom and by the idea of endless form filling. If you *are* considering doing it yourself, you should first consult one of the specialist conveyancing publications.

Conveyancing in Scotland

In Scotland, the conveyancing system is totally different and, some say, much fairer to prospective buyers. Perhaps the most important difference is that the purchase does not hinge on the exchange of contracts, remaining 'subject to contract' for some considerable time. Instead, a prospective buyer makes an offer through his solicitors in the form of a 'sealed bid' auction. If the seller accepts the offer he is bound by law to sell at the agreed price and the buyer is also bound to the deal. This system of 'concluded missives' means that agreement is reached quickly and the sale can be concluded in the space of a few days.

Two important points to note about this system are, first, that because the missives are signed by the solicitors for seller and buyer, you may not actually have to sign anything personally. Secondly, the missives will specify a 'date of entry' (which is effectively the day on which you can take possession of the property) and although there is no fixed time scale between the conclusion of missives and date of entry, the average period is six to eight weeks.

One drawback of this system is that each person interested in buying a particular property will need to have a survey carried out *before* submitting an offer. If there are several people interested in a property, the selling agent will usually fix a closing date at which time all parties must submit their 'best' offer on price and likely completion date. The seller will usually pick the highest bid, but he is not actually bound to accept the highest or for that matter any offer. So, in the event that you are a would-be buyer and you have been

unsuccessful in a number of bids, the cost of your surveys
will mount up.

Although some properties are advertised on the basis of a
fixed price, the majority of adverts for Scottish houses ask for
'offers over' a specific figure. Obviously the exact price
achieved depends on market forces and so it is not possible
to give a precise idea of how much more than the asking price
a prospective buyer should bid. If the market is quiet and
there is only one potential buyer, there may be room for
negotiation. Although this system is criticised as inflationary
in the sense that the buyer may pay more than he needs to,
each potential buyer should have considered with his solicitor
how much the property is worth.

Completion of the sale

In the time between conclusion of missives and the agreed
date of entry, solicitors for each side will carry through the
conveyancing procedure. This involves checking the title,
carrying out all the necessary searches, preparing and
executing the required disposition which transfers ownership,
and also executing the standard security (ie the mortgage).

To complete the sale, the buyer's solicitor presents a cheque
for the agreed price and the seller's solicitor delivers the keys,
plus the disposition transferring ownership, together with the
relevant title deeds. The seller's solicitor also delivers a letter
of obligation which protects the buyer during the time it takes
for the title to be re-registered.

After this settlement, the buyer's solicitor must lodge the
disposition and the standard security with the relevant register.
In Scotland there are currently two systems of land
registration.

The newer system is the Land Register of Scotland which
involves ownership of the property being defined on the
Ordnance Survey map with the rights and burdens being

declared in a formal land certificate which is guaranteed by the Keeper of the Land Register (on behalf of the State). Currently, this system only operates in the Glasgow and surrounding areas but eventually it will cover the whole of Scotland. The older system involves the Register of Sasines which is a register of title deeds as opposed to a guaranteed register of title. Both of these are public registers.

Although there are some leasehold titles in Scotland, they are very rare and the leases concerned normally run for several hundred years.

As soon as you find a property in Scotland which you like, contact your solicitor who will 'note an interest' with the selling agent. The agent will not sell the property without giving you the opportunity to make an offer. Your solicitor will keep you informed of closing dates and ensure you obtain a surveyor's report in time to make your offer.

Licensed conveyancing

Until recently, solicitors more or less had a monopoly on conveyancing services for housebuyers. This is now being eroded by the increasing numbers of people who do it themselves and by the emergence of licenced conveyancers. A licensed conveyancer offers substantially the same conveyancing service as a solicitor, and is experienced at conveyancing, but is not officially qualified as a solicitor. Using such a firm may well be cheaper than using a solicitor, but if you are tempted to use such a firm, check that it is a member of the National Association of Conveyancers. It's also worth bearing in mind that while you may wish to use a licensed conveyancer, most lenders still prefer to instruct solicitors to act on their own behalf. This could therefore reduce the apparent saving to you.

There are currently no licensed conveyancers operating in

Scotland. The vast majority of people use a solicitor and it is extremely rare that anyone carries through the conveyancing themselves. Traditionally, house selling is dealt with by solicitors grouped together in a locality to form Solicitors' Property Centres. If you are looking to buy in a particular area of Scotland, check to see whether there is a local SPC as well as contacting local estate agents.

Useful contacts

Law Society – Tel: 01–242 1222
Law Society of Scotland – Tel: 031–226 7411
Solicitors Complaints Bureau – Tel: 01–834 2288
National Association of Conveyancers – Tel: 01–405 8582

6 Home buying and financial planning

Introduction

Having purchased your home, one of the most important steps in your financial planning is to protect it. This protection takes three forms:

1 Having invested a substantial sum of money in an asset, you've got to look after it. Make sure it's fully protected and duly insured and make sure you keep it in good repair.
2 Having taken on a substantial debt, you need to protect your family so that the debt can be paid off if you're not around to pay it off yourself.
3 Having committed yourself to a regular series of payments in the future (which can only be paid out of income), you should be protecting this income at times when you can't work (through illness or disability) or when you no longer wish to work (when you retire).

There is no doubt that buying a house, whether it's for the first time or not, is going to burn a big hole in your pocket. It's the major investment of your life and there are so many incidental costs that you could be forgiven for trying to cut some of the corners. Most people struggle with their finances during the purchase, and some attempt to cut corners, by cutting back on contents insurances, for example. These may be short term savings, but they are potentially disastrous.

Property insurance

Having worked hard to buy and furnish your house, it makes little sense to leave it unprotected – the risk of something happening to your property is surprisingly high. Each year, roughly 10% of houses in the United Kingdom are broken into and many thousands of homes suffer from fires, often caused by untended cookers. Some families are left with nothing when their house is gutted by fire: no possessions and no compensation.

When you take out your insurance, it's up to you to make sure you have enough cover. If you don't you could end up having your claims 'averaged'. Many people assume this will only happen if they make a *total* claim on all their property or possessions but it will also apply to partial claims. For example, if your kitchen was gutted by fire and your insurer established that you had only insured your property for two thirds of its true value, then you would only get two thirds of the cost of putting your kitchen to rights. With fitted kitchens costing what they do today, this could leave you with a hefty bill to make up the difference. Apart from providing the roof over your head, it is also worth remembering that your home is probably one of the largest investments you will ever make. Rising residential property values over the years have ensured homeowners a good return on their money. So it is an investment worth protecting. Don't forget that each year about one in ten policy holders claim on their house buildings policy with weather and water damage top of the list for claims followed by subsidence and, lastly, fire.

The cost of rebuilding

One of the most common points of confusion when people are insuring their home is over the difference between the market value and the rebuilding cost of the property. One simple illustration of this is to consider two identical properties, one overlooking a park and the other overlooking the local rubbish tip. The rebuilding costs will be the same but the market value definitely won't.

If you want to make your own estimate of the rebuilding cost of your property, send for a free copy of the Association of British Insurers leaflet, *Building Insurance for Homeowners* which gives average rebuilding costs per square foot for different types and ages of property in different parts of the country. It is obtainable by sending a stamped addressed envelope to the ABI, Aldermary House, Queen Street, London, EC4N 1TT.

Working out the square footage of your house is simple enough (but don't forget, it refers to the square footage of living accommodation so if you have a two-storey house as distinct from a bungalow, you have to double the house floor area to get the square footage). Once you have arrived at the total area, multiply that by the appropriate 'per square foot' building cost and you have your answer. But you will also have to add on an allowance for the cost of rebuilding your garage and other outbuildings, walls and fences.

If your home is double glazed, or has superior kitchen or sanitary fittings or high quality wall and floor finishes, you are recommended to add up to 25% to your total sum insured. Compare your final figure with your existing property cover and top-up if necessary. Most insurers now index-link their home buildings policies but don't forget that if you improve your home or add an extension this will increase the rebuilding cost and you should review your cover.

Getting your home insured

It is very important that you do something about insurance for the property (and its contents) before you take possession of your home. Your solicitor will probably organise buildings cover for the property prior to completion if you haven't already done so yourself (but do check). He is less likely to have arranged contents cover unless you specifically ask him.

Insurance premiums vary from company to company so that it may well be worthwhile shopping around. Most lenders will usually have a short list of borrowers with whom they have negotiated terms and you will be asked to use one of these but it's up to you to choose which one. If, however, your house insurance is down to you, then you can either get it direct from your building society or bank, through your usual financial adviser or through a high-street broker. Try to get a range of quotations so that you end up with the best choice.

Do read the small print – the last ten years have seen some remarkable fluctuations in the British climate with subsidence caused by the extremely dry weather of 1976 being replaced by 'heave' as the rainfall pattern resumed its usual inexorable course. In addition, we've had some extremely harsh winters in recent years and, of course, most recently, the hurricane winds of 1987. You may find that what appears to be a relatively cheap house policy turns out to have some restrictions in these areas so read it carefully.

Your possessions

It is estimated that nearly one in four households in the country still have no contents cover at all and of those that do, two-thirds are under-insured. Given that the incidence of burglary is increasing each year, more and more people are running risks. Not surprisingly, therefore, the cost of insuring your contents is likely to vary across the country and you will obviously pay more to insure a house in a major town, be it London or Leeds, than you will in rural areas. In order to keep claims down and give householders an incentive to take extra precautions, some insurance companies are now starting to offer discounts to those who install secure locks and burglar alarms. If you have fitted these yourself, make sure your insurance company is aware of this because you may be eligible for a discount on the premiums. Another way of keeping your premiums down is to say that you will pay part of each claim yourself.

When you're enquiring about contents cover, you must specify if you want insurance for particular items such as jewellery, cameras, your rare collection of old 78's and so on. Bear in mind also that if you work from home using equipment such as a typewriter or a home computer, you will need to take out extra insurance as the 'tools of your trade' will usually not be covered by an ordinary home contents policy.

Like buildings cover, most contents insurances are also index-linked but once again, if you acquire more possessions, it's up to you to keep a check on the level of cover and to adjust it if necessary.

A standard 'new for old' contents policy will specify cover for the usual things such as fire and theft and may also cover against things like flood and hurricane damage. You can also get accidental damage cover which will cover you in case you kick a pot of paint over the carpet whilst decorating the dining room.

Indemnity insurance

Cheaper policies are available for people who might find it too expensive to pay for a full 'new for old' policy, perhaps elderly people who might not have too many possessions to insure. These are called indemnity policies and for the lower premiums you get less cover. Instead of new for old, the insurance company takes into account the wear and tear an item has suffered, paying compensation accordingly. You need to know what is meant by 'wear and tear' so don't plump for the cheapest quote without checking the policy exclusions first.

At the other end of the price scale there are 'all risks' policies which, contrary to their implication, do not cover everything. But they are as comprehensive as such policies get, including cover for items used outside the home such as video cameras, bicycles and lawn mowers. If you lose your camera on holiday, you can normally claim for it under an all risks policy.

Finally, do check your contents insurance regularly because it's surprising just how quickly the cost of replacing your contents changes over a period of time. Most households continually add to their possessions and merely to index-link your cover is rarely enough. Get into the habit of reviewing your contents insurance every time you pay your renewal premium.

Home and family

It is often interesting to see just how people's plans revolve around their ability to earn money. Very rarely do they think about what might happen if they were unable to earn a living and yet it is relatively simple to protect yourself against that possibility. To some extent you probably do. Most people give up some of their income now in return for an income sometime in the future. That's what a pension is for. But what is equally important is to consider the other sorts of circumstances where it makes equally good sense to put aside some of your income now to guarantee the means of providing an income in the future.

For the homebuyer, loss of income is potentially catastrophic. Not only is there a mortgage to pay off but the day-to-day expenses of owning and running a home can be high as well. To take on this kind of long term commitment without at the same time providing the means to fulfill these commitments if the worst happens is not good financial planning.

For our purposes, there are two events which can cut the income off at a stroke; the first is death and the second is disablement through illness or accident. The means of protecting yourself (and your dependants) from these two unwelcome visitors are life assurance and permanent health insurance.

Protection for your family

Just consider what life assurance is. It's the only way of ensuring that a predictable sum of money will be available at a totally unpredictable time in the future. For that reason, if you are just married or if you have just decided to start a family, you should also think about buying some life assurance. Because buying a home is such a big thing, it is important to consider it as part of a wider development of your financial affairs, especially if you have dependants. Although it is best if both husband and wife have policies on each other's lives, if only one of them is the breadwinner, he or she should certainly have a policy to benefit the other.

The cheapest form of life assurance is called term assurance. A man in his late twenties could get £50,000 worth of life cover for less than the cost of a packet of cigarettes a week, and giving up those cigarettes could involve a double level of cost-saving because for non-smokers (and women) the rates are often even cheaper.

Varieties of term assurance

There are various types of term assurance to suit different circumstances. For instance, we referred in a previous chapter to mortgage protection, which is term assurance to cover the to mortgage repayments if you should die before it is paid off. Family income benefit is another type. This will

pay out a regular income to your beneficiaries, rather than
a lump sum.

Convertible term assurance is probably the most popular type,
because it offers you the chance to change the policy to an
endowment or 'whole of life' policy at a later stage, without
medical evidence. The thing to remember about term
assurance is that you don't get any money back from it if you
don't die during the period the policy is in force. That's why
it is so cheap.

Endowment and whole of life assurance

If not getting anything back seems a bit of a raw deal, perhaps
you should consider taking out an endowment or whole of
life policy (with-profits or unit-linked) right from the start.
The difference between the two is quite simple. Both provide
a guaranteed level of life cover but an endowment policy has
a maturity date. At this time, the policy provides a cash sum
equal to the life cover and this is the reason why endowment
policies are used for mortgage repayment. A whole of life
policy, on the other hand, provides life cover for as long as
you want to continue paying the contributions, with a small
cash value as well which will build up over the years.

The principle is the same as with term assurance; you are
saving money now to provide funds for your family (or just
your spouse) should you die prematurely. The sum assured
(the proceeds from the policy) goes to your dependants for
use either to settle a large debt ie a mortgage or for investment
to provide a replacement income. On the other hand, in the
happy event that you are still alive and kicking at some time
in the future, you will see some (if not all) of your money
back plus bonuses or whatever profits the insurance company
has made on the investments.

However, do bear in mind with life assurance policies that

although they are a good way of building up a lump sum for the future, they are designed for protection over the *long term* (ten years or more). There are more efficient ways of saving if you anticipate using the proceeds in only about five years' time.

As pointed out in the earlier chapter about mortgages, life assurance policies with investment links are many and varied. If you decide to take out such a policy, your main concern should be to check that the company whose policy you are buying can prove a consistently good return over a number of years. Although past performance is no guarantee of the future, it gives you a good idea of which companies are the most reliable. Get hold of a copy of the magazine *Money Management* which contains up to date figures for all unit-linked funds spanning at least ten years.

Permanent health insurance

Permanent health insurance is another form of income protection. Instead of paying out if you die, this type of cover compensates you and your family if you, as the breadwinner, are taken seriously ill or injured for a long period, even permanently to the extent that you can no longer work. For the housebuyer, a lengthy period off work could be a very serious matter indeed.

The chances of your being unable to work through illness or disability are higher than you might think. For the average family man, the chances of his being off work for a month due to illness in any twelve month period are about 15 times *higher* than his chances of dying in that year. At any one time, over half a million men are off work and have been off work for at least six months due to illness. Of these, nearly half have been off work for at least three years.

Permanent health insurance (PHI) is one of the most

underrated areas of financial planning, which is odd because illness and disability do occur with considerable frequency. Most sick pay schemes only provide a continued income for a limited period. The self-employed usually have *no* alternative source of income and for them prolonged illness could be quite disastrous. The State benefits are barely adequate. A PHI policy will provide a replacement income for as long as you're off sick and it will normally be a percentage of your previous earnings. The amount you have to pay for this kind of cover will usually depend on your occupation but will also depend on whether you want your replacement income to start one, three, six or twelve months after your disability and whether or not you want to index-link your benefits. To take a simple example, a man aged 40 could receive an income of up to £500 a month from six months after falling ill until he is 60 for a PHI premium of just £12 a month. The benefit of £500 a month would pay the repayments on a mortgage up to, say, £60,000.

Pension planning for the future

A frequent question, particularly at retirement, is, 'Should we pay off the mortgage?' The question is often an emotional rather than a practical one. In some cases, because of the tax relief on the interest, it would be possible to earn a better return by investing the capital elsewhere. However, that all depends on whether or not you have enough income to continue paying the monthly repayments ie is your pension adequate?

Retirement will normally be the first time that many of us have the opportunity to be totally independent – but the quality of this independence will depend upon the plans that we've made. The amount of cash that we need to accumulate by the age of 60 or 65 in order to provide an income for at least the next 15 to 20 years is substantial and it needs careful planning. For people in employment, the planning is largely done for them. They will often belong to a company pension scheme but a large number do not and in this respect they're in the same position as the self-employed. It's up to them to make their own plans.

Pensions for employees

Even if you are an employee, your maximum pension is limited to two-thirds of your final salary. That, however, is subject to a whole range of Inland Revenue rules (in addition to the rules of your own pension scheme) and you may well find that the projected pension at the age you intend to retire is a good deal lower than you imagine. In today's mobile world, most employees *cannot* automatically look forward to a maximum pension – it's up to you to find out what pension you can expect and to do something about it.

Fortunately, successive Governments have recognised the need for pension provision and there does appear to be general agreement, regardless of political persuasion, that it should be encouraged. This normally takes the form of tax incentives on the money going into a retirement plan, favourable tax treatment of the investment while it's there and beneficial treatment of the income coming out (with the understandable condition that you can't take the money until retirement age).

For people in company schemes the way is now open to them to improve their company pension by making their own additional personal arrangements (called Additional Voluntary Contributions – or AVCs for short). You can put in up to 15% of your salary and it's fully tax deductable. It's a good way to prepare for the future.

Pensions for the self-employed

If you're self-employed, (or if you haven't got a company pension scheme), then your financial plans are entirely up to you. There's no restriction on the level of pension you can provide for yourself and you can pay up to 17.5% of your earnings (and even more if you're older) to a personal pension scheme. You also have a further advantage in that you can make up for past contributions over the last six years.

Don't forget that for the self-employed, personal pension planning is absolutely vital because they *only* have the basic old age pension to look forward to and no earlier than the State retirement age. The message from successive Governments has been quite clear – help yourself, because nobody else is going to.

Pensions in the future

Although it's beyond the scope of this book, it is important that you bring yourself up to date with the new legislation on pensions. In July 1988, a whole new era of pensions legislation was introduced and more than ever before the emphasis is on the individual making his own plans for the future. One of the key state pensions for employed people the State Earnings Related Pensions Scheme (SERPS) has been amended and the eventual benefits for most employed people will be much lower than the level of intended benefits when the scheme was first introduced in 1978.

At the same time, the government is offering incentives to all employed people to make provision for their own retirement planning and you should make quite sure that you are familiar with the legislation and that you get competent financial advice on what is the best way forward for you personally.

Paying off your mortgage

When you finally retire, and your pension is being paid out, you will normally receive a tax-free cash lump sum. If you have

taken out a pension-related mortgage, then this will be used
to pay off your mortgage, but if you haven't (for example,
you may have taken out a lifetime loan as covered earlier in
the book) then you now have the means to pay off the
mortgage if you wish.

But should you? In many cases, it will be more of an emotional
decision than a financial one. The idea of getting rid of your
biggest debt can often seem attractive, particularly if you are
no longer earning. But do think about it, because a mortgage
represents the cheapest form of borrowing and you may be
able to invest your cash lump sum in a better form of
investment. Don't forget that once you pay off your mortgage,
you will not be able to take advantage of a loan with tax-
free interest until you are old enough to qualify for a Home
Income Plan (see Chapter 10) and that could be some time
away.

Making a Will

This may seem an odd section to have in a book on buying a
home but it is an area which cannot be ignored by the
homeowner. It's all tied up with inheritance tax planning, one
of the basic rules being that everything left to your spouse
does not attract any liability to inheritance tax at all. In
general, if you die, and leave your entire estate to your wife/
husband, then no inheritance tax is payable. When, however,
your wife/husband dies and leaves the estate to your children,
that is when the inheritance tax burden comes home to roost.

Many people get mixed up about this. They believe that
because there is no inheritance tax to pay this means that
the entire estate *automatically* passes to the wife or husband.
In reality, *nothing* could be further from the truth. The *only*
way that you can guarantee that everything passes to your
spouse is to make a Will. It often comes as a surprise to
financial planners to find the number of people who haven't

made a Will. What people cannot imagine is the chaos and distress they can leave behind them when they die because they have left no clear, legally enforceable instructions as to how they wish their property to be divided up once it passes from their ownership.

That's what a Will is. Its purpose is very simple and straightforward. It is a document which expresses in clear terms exactly what you wish to happen to your property when you die. It isn't a legal requirement to use a solicitor but it is strongly recommended that you *always* use the services of a solicitor when drawing up your Will. This ensures that it will be drafted in absolutely unambiguous (though not necessarily simple) terms which will then leave no doubt at all as to how you wish your property to be divided up when you die.

Intestacy

If you die without leaving a Will (which is known as dying 'intestate') it may be that certain of your intended beneficiaries will be unable to claim for *any* part of your estate, no matter how deserving they may be and no matter what promises you have made them. Your *principal* beneficiaries ie your wife and immediate family are protected because the law will ensure that they get certain shares. However, the courts don't have the time or the resources to consider each case on its merits and your estate will be distributed among your family according to the 'intestacy rules'.

The laws of intestacy are an ideal breeding ground for family disputes. If you leave more than £75,000 and you don't make a Will, your wife will *only* inherit everything if you have no children or grandchildren. If you leave more than £125,000 your wife will only get everything if both your parents are dead and you have no brothers, sisters, nephews or nieces. In the 'worst' case, the surviving spouse is only entitled to the personal effects, a statutory legacy of £75,000 and the income for life from one *half* of the rest of the estate.

For the purposes of the homeowner, it's important to know that ownership of the house *does not pass automatically* to the surviving spouse. All that your spouse can do (provided he or she was living in the house at the time and that it was owned by you) is to require that the house is given to her in settlement of her legal rights under the intestacy rules. If the house is worth more than £75,000, then she might have a problem. The solution is simple – make a Will.

Conclusion

Buying a home is a major financial transaction and it is important to put it into perspective. Concentrating too much on this one area of finance and ignoring the other areas, could lead you to make decisions which might be difficult to recover from in later years. To concentrate all your resources on your home at the expense of ignoring other areas of financial planning such as life assurance and your pension, could mean having to give up your home at some point in the future because, owing to circumstances entirely outside your control, you are no longer able to earn the income which will enable you to continue to live in it.

7 The selling process

If you have bought well, you shouldn't have any trouble selling. Your selling preparations should include a list of the repairs and cosmetic changes required, an investigation of prices being fetched by other similar properties in the area, and a decision on when you are going to put the property on the market. The spring and early summer months are traditionally the most active in the property market. Aim to sell during this period in order that your home is seen by as many people as possible.

Maximising the value of your home

People buy on the basis of what they see. Though your property may be potentially marvellous, if it is untidy, poorly lit and in need of decoration you will probably be disappointed by the response from people who come to view it. If you do receive an offer, it may well be less than you are willing to accept. Even if you are sick of the place, you shouldn't allow this to colour your judgment when it comes to selling. Your only concern should be to get as much for it as you can.

By the same token, the lived-in look will add value because it will appear that you have made a good home. Potential buyers can easily picture themselves living in this situation. It's all psychological and you are simply trying to convince people that your property is exactly what they are looking for. A tidy, fully-furnished house or flat will fetch much more than an empty one, even if it is exactly the same. One rather bizarre idea is that you should get the smell of your house 'arranged' to give that cosy lived-in feel. A suggestion much favoured by estate agents is that you should arrange to have some freshly ground coffee being brewed or some freshly baked rolls in the oven whenever your potential buyer comes to visit. This combination of aromas is alleged to induce a sense of well-being in even the most hardened househunter. It's worth a try!

To avoid being knocked down from your original asking price, you should make sure the decor is as good as it can be and, above all, keep the place clean. Fix your faulty door latches and sticky windows and keep hinges oiled. If potential buyers are viewing it in the evening, it should be warm and well lit.

Improvements to consider

Home improvements are all the rage in this era of gentrification and redevelopment, but some do not add any lasting value to a property. Generally speaking, the more extravagant the home improvement, the less likely you are to recoup the cost of it when you come to sell. Most buyers would rather have an extra room than a swimming pool or a sauna. Concentrate on more modest home improvements that will put those crucial extra thousands on your profit.

There are specific improvements you should consider. The general decor must look as if you have taken some care of it. A simple thing like a new coat of paint could transform the barest of walls. The most important rooms in any house are arguably the kitchen and the bathroom. Contrary to what the so-called specialists tell you, however, it is not necessary to spend £5,000 to improve your kitchen. For a few hundred pounds you can transform any room. If there is a DIY cash and carry near you, take a look around it once you have a vague idea of how you want the room to look. The basic materials (doors, worktops, shelving etc) will cost you very little. Draw up a few ideas of how you would like it to look and then call up some local carpenters to give you a quotation for fitting them if you cannot do it yourself.

Are you sure you want to sell?

Moving house is probably the last thing you want to be doing at a time when your finances are being stretched by the arrival of children. This is another reason for the popularity of home improvements. Many people would rather add an extra room or an extension to the back of the house than suffer the stresses and strains of selling and looking for a bigger one.

If you need cash for the job, tell your lender you would like a further advance on your mortgage, or alternatively a home improvement loan. Assuming that your income has grown since you took out the mortgage, you should not experience any resistance from the lender. They will want to make a fresh valuation of the house to ensure that its value covers the increased loan and that what you are planning is not going to ruin the resale value of the property. The lender may have a better idea of the likely cost of your improvements, having dealt with many similar cases. They may even be able to put you in touch with a reliable firm of builders, who have done good work for other clients. Further information on raising extra cash can be found in Chapter 2.

Getting the best from your estate agent

The basic service that an estate agent will provide to you as a seller involves marketing your property to an audience that includes those people who already live in the area but want to move, and those people who want to move into the area from elsewhere. Your property's details may be included with many others in local press advertisements, and you may get a picture of it in the agent's window. Details will also be sent to all the people who contact the agency for a list of property in the area.

Agents' commission is anything from 1.5% to 3.5%. It averages out at 2.5% but could be less if you grant sole agency to one firm, assuming you feel confident that the property will sell quickly. Currently in London you will pay as much as 3.5% commission to your estate agent, which works out at £3,500 (plus VAT) on a house sold for £100,000. In other parts of the country, estate agents' commission averages out at somewhere between 1.75% and 2%. That's good money for the limited effort expended by most agents on behalf of their smaller clients and one reason why insurance companies, banks and building societies have been so keen to grab a major share of this market.

Most people begrudge paying their estate agent's fee but the agent cannot win. If the property is sold quickly they feel the agent hasn't earned his money, but if it is not under offer after a month they feel they have been neglected. It is important, therefore, that you have an idea of how marketable your property is to give you some means of negotiating your estate agent's fee up-front.

Before you choose an estate agent

Here are a few things you can do before deciding on an estate agent:

1   Look very carefully at your own property. Make sure you know its true value and decide on the level of marketing needed to sell it.
2   Make a thorough investigation of the local estate agents. Talk to people in the area who have sold and count the 'For sale' and 'Sold' boards to give you an idea of which agents are selling the most property.
3   Look at the quality of agents' advertising in the local

press. For most people, the choice comes down to gut
feeling – you decide you like the way a firm presents itself.
4   Don't choose an agent simply because he has given you
the highest valuation of your property. Anybody can get
an instruction by telling you your property is worth
£10,000 more than it is and then you'll wonder why
nobody wants to buy it. However, if this high valuation
tallies with your own view of current prices, the agent's
commission is acceptable or negotiable and you are
confident that the price is attainable, appoint the agent.

Having decided that you are going to pay the estate agent to
sell your property and to act exclusively in your interests,
there are various ways in which your estate agent can act for
you.

Sole agency This is where you place your property for sale
with one firm of estate agents. You may do this with or
without a sole agency *agreement*, (under which you undertake,
for a specified period of time, not to instruct any other agent
to sell the same property for you). Under sole agency, you
don't have to pay any commission if you sell the property
yourself – for example, through a personal contact or by
advertising the property yourself. However, if sole agency is
granted with *sole selling rights*, then you will have to pay
commission to the agent however the property is sold.

Don't agree to give sole agency without at least a 1% discount
because, contrary to the estate agent's argument that sole
agency encourages him to make a greater effort, it could
simply encourage complacency because he knows he has got
the commission in the bag as long as the property sells.

Joint sole agency This is where you can instruct two agents
to act for you in co-operation with each other. The
commission (which *may* be more than that payable to a single
sole agent) is shared between them, regardless of which one
actually sells your house.

Sub-agency This is where you place the property for sale with one or more principal agents who then appoint one or more sub-agents to co-operate with them in the disposal of the property. The point here is that the estate agent has no authority to appoint a sub-agent without your permission. It won't cost you any more if you do – your principal agents will share any resulting commission with the sub-agents.

Multiple agency This is where you place the property for sale with two or more agents separately and the whole of the commission is payable to whichever agent sells the house, with the others receiving nothing at all. In the meantime, if you succeed in selling the house yourself, you won't normally have to pay commission to any of the agents you have instructed.

The most common forms of estate agency are sole agency and multiple agency with multiple agency being rather more common in London and the South of England.

Larger properties

It is only in the sale of large and prestigious properties where the services of an estate agent are vital. It's a specialised market and estate agents know not only the best places to advertise, but they may also have wealthy clients waiting for a particular mansion or country house to come onto the market. In the case of a large residential house with its own estate, the agent will contact foreign buyers and place advertisements in glossy magazines such as *Country Life*, where a full page advertisement costs upwards of £2,000.

The concentration of estate agency business in the hands of major national companies does not mean the service will be getting any cheaper. In fact it could turn out to be more expensive. It is quite likely that the large firms will polish up and round out their range of insurance and other financial services on offer within estate agency offices. In these circumstances, they could comfortably charge higher commissions in the knowledge that they are providing a comprehensive package.

In this environment there may in theory be room for the smaller estate agent to undercut the big boys. But the small independent will not survive by simply cutting commission rates. Small firms offering a cheap service will only attract small and cheap properties, so they will be getting a smaller slice of a smaller cake. The future of the supermarket estate agency package is also uncertain because it's difficult to offer a good agency service for £100 a house, which is a fairly standard charge.

Selling it yourself

If you live in an area of great demand, you might not even need the services of an estate agent. The most essential thing is that you don't sell yourself short. Be confident that the asking price is correct and ask someone you know who is good with words to draft a snappy advertisement.

1   If you know how much the property is worth, advertise privately in your local paper.
2   If you want to know roughly how much your property is worth, ask two or three agents to come and give you a valuation. They will probably pester you to let them sell it, but you'll just have to put up with that.
3   Use the small ads in the quality national newspapers, especially the Sunday papers, if you want to achieve a wider market.
4   Don't be bullied by local agents who have seen you advertising privately and who call up telling you it's a big mistake!

Speeding up the sale

There are a number of things you can do yourself which could
help to speed up the selling process. Having hopefully attracted
a number of potential buyers, what can you do to help them
make a decision?

A CV of your house If you were looking for a job, you would
probably prepare a curriculum vitae which would help a
potential employer decide whether or not you were worth
interviewing for the position. So, why not apply the same
principle to your house. If *you* were looking for a house for
yourself, what things would be of interest to you? Proximity
to the shops? Access to the nearest large city? Local schools?

Put yourself in the mind of potential buyers and provide a
list of answers to the questions they might put to you. You
might be selling the family home because now that the
children have grown up, it has become too big for you. But
it is a home for a *family* and your buyer could well have
children of school age. It could well be worth your while
finding out some details of local schools to help your buyer
make a decision.

It's your house so don't be afraid to 'sell' it!

House dimensions If you sell your house through an estate
agent, they will come and measure your house and include
details in the house particulars. Without actually seeing the
house (or even after seeing it), the buyer has to try and work
out exactly what '21ft by 12ft 6ins (into inglenook) with ante-
room leading into spacious hall (13ft by 11ft at widest point)'
actually means.

You can measure your own house and provide a floor plan.
If you draw it on squared paper, you can provide an accurate
representation of what your house is actually like. Most
builders provide this when selling a new house but very few

estate agents use the same idea to speed up the sale of an old house. It could just make all the difference and, if you ask the estate agent to include it in the house details, you may attract a few more potential buyers.

Photography Your house will look its best in the sunshine with the flowers in bloom and with leaves on the trees. Take photographs of your house and garden from as many angles as possible in the summer. Nothing looks better on a house advertisement than an attractive colour photograph of the property being offered for sale and nothing looks worse than a dingy picture taken in a hurry in poor light in late February as you rush to get your house on the market for Easter. Be prepared. Have a good stock of photographs and ask your estate agent to use them.

Local search In Chapter 5 we mentioned doing your own local search together with some of the problems associated with it. If you are buying a house, your lender isn't going to take too much notice of the search that you do yourself and the same is true when selling. Your buyer's lender isn't going to take any notice at all of any search that you've carried out but it could be worth your while finding out *some* information from your local authority about plans for the area. You can always ask to see the plans for future developments near you and this could help you deal with any awkward questions. If a road is going to be built close by, there's no point in hiding the fact because the buyer's solicitor will find out anyway. If you know what is going on yourself, you will be in a better position to deal with any problems. After all, you don't want to find out from a potential buyer (or rather, a one-time potential buyer) that a new building development or the new M99 motorway will be next to your house.

At a time of rapidly moving house prices, it can be easy to sell a house – at a price. What you want is the *best* price for your house but to achieve this you must be prepared to do some spadework yourself and not expect the estate agent to deal with it all for you. Remember, that an extra £2,000 could make all the difference to you and not a great deal to him.

8 Your second home

As a nation, we are getting more affluent and second home ownership is becoming increasingly popular. After filling up our first home with the increasing range of 'necessities' (video recorder, microwave oven etc) and with the second car in the garage, a home in the country, or even overseas, is for many people the ultimate luxury.

There are a number of different ways to buy an alternative property, whether you want a holiday retreat or a retirement home. The thing to bear in mind is that you don't have to be rich to own two homes. However, you do need to have your wits about you and it is essential that you have the help of an accountant and a solicitor to insure against costly mistakes.

By and large, buying a second home in this country is no different to buying a first home. You will go through exactly the same process of buying and you will use the same specialist help.

The financial side will be a little more tricky. Unless you buy your home for cash, you will need to borrow it and most lenders will be rather more cautious when lending money on a second property. You may well have to pay a slightly higher rate of interest on your loan.

You may decide to borrow against your existing assets such as your house, your life assurance policies and any valuables you may possess. Bear in mind when estimating how much you can borrow, that the lender will only be willing to grant you a percentage of their value. For example, say you have had your house valued at £80,000 and you still have a

£30,000 mortgage outstanding. You can only borrow against the £50,000 worth of free equity and you won't be offered the full amount. Expect to be offered in the region of 80 per cent assuming property prices are stable.

Similarly, let's assume that the current surrender value on your life assurance policy is £10,000. You can only really count on half this amount for a loan, especially if the policy is linked to the price of shares or property, as a unit-linked policy is. A good unit-linked policy is as secure as any form of life assurance but the shock of recent share price movements has instilled caution in the minds of most lenders. The reason they won't give you the full amount is because they know that nothing in business life is ever guaranteed and that you may be forced to sell one of these assets quickly (and cheaply) to raise much needed cash.

On the tax position, you will not generally get any tax relief on the interest on any money that you borrow to buy your second home in the United Kingdom. The only exceptions to this are if the house has been purchased by a dependent relative (you will find more details on this in Chapter 10) or if the property is being used for holiday letting (you will find more details about that in Chapter 9). If the second home is for your use only, then you can forget about tax relief.

You won't be able to forget about capital gains tax because a *second* home is not exempt, whereas your *main* residence is (although, once again, there is a special condition regarding dependent relatives which is explained in Chapter 10). However, you do have the choice of deciding which is to be regarded as your main residence if you buy a second home. You should take professional advice on this but generally speaking choose as your main residence the property which is likely to increase in value the most. When you buy your second home, you have only two years from the date of purchase to decide which is to be your main residence. If you haven't decided by then, the Revenue will decide for you and they will usually choose your first home to be your main residence.

Buying property abroad

The growth in overseas property buying in recent years has been quite staggering and not just from the point of view of the United Kingdom. The general increase in prosperity throughout Europe has meant that more and more people from Northern Europe are looking for a holiday or retirement home in the sunnier parts of Southern Europe. The Mediterranean coastline is now dotted with apartments and villas with Spain being the favourite spot at the moment (Southern Spain is rapidly becoming a form of 'Europolis' on account of the number of different nationalities who are making their home there – and it is also being given the rather unkind homily, 'Spain will be very nice – when it's finished').

Compared to buying property in the United Kingdom, buying abroad seems to be simplicity itself. There are no end of people in the United Kingdom eager to sell you property abroad and they will even fly you out there and put you up in a hotel at their expense. Provided you are prepared to limit your search in this way there are a number of reputable agencies who will provide you with an excellent service. But be *warned*. Buying your property in, for example, Spain may appear to be little different to buying property in England when you are having it explained to you in a hotel in Tunbridge Wells. However, the reality is:

1 You are buying a house in a foreign country.
2 The contract may be in a foreign language.
3 The legal system is *totally* different.
4 Spain still has exchange control on monies taken out of the country.
5 The Spanish bureaucracy can seem almost medieval at times.
6 Spain has a different tax system.

Provided you follow the rules, you will have no problems.

But *don't* cut corners, and be prepared to pay for expert advice and help. Why omit to do things that you wouldn't dream of forgetting to do if you were buying a home in the United Kingdom? You expect to pay a solicitor to ensure that all the legalities are tied up but some people still buy houses in Spain without a thought for the legal niceties. It would be beyond belief if it didn't happen.

The financial position

In addition to taking care on the legal side, take care on the financial side:

1   Don't over-commit yourself either on the purchase price or the running costs. Remember, in addition to coping with domestic inflation, you now have to cope with the fluctuating exchange rate and a foreign inflation rate.
2   Make sure you pay for your property in the correct way. Many countries still have exchange control and you want to be able to get your money out when you sell the property.
3   Don't overlook the tax position. If you own a second house in this country, you will have to take due regard of capital gains tax, inheritance tax and, if you let your property, income tax. The same will be true in a foreign country so you need to make yourself fully familiar with their tax rules as well.

The likely costs

Follow the same guidelines we used at the start to establish what you want from the property (sea-view, golf course, skiing, walks?). Let us assume that you would like to buy a house on the Mediterranean coast. A villa with three bedrooms and swimming pool in Mijas will cost about £100,000. On the 'frontline' in Marbella, a luxurious two bedroom apartment will set you back at least £130,000. Up the coast in the Costa Brava or the Costa Blanca, you will pay a more modest £70,000 for a two or three bedroom villa.

A French chateau might set you back as much as £250,000, but a small apartment in a ski-resort would only be £50,000. Add to these prices another 10% to cover the cost of legal fees and local property taxes, plus a bit for any renovations and improvements you might need to make before you can move in. Bear in mind there may also be recurring charges such as annual maintenance, insurance and rates. So you could easily end up spending 20% on top of the purchase price.

If you are buying a second property as an investment, you should buy into the most popular areas, or as near as you can. Resale values in the more remote regions of Europe are unpredictable at the best of times and they don't follow the fortunes of the domestic economy the way British prices do. In terms of location, the Costa del Sol is the obvious choice in Spain. Similarly, the Cote d'Azur or anything within striking distance of Paris is the obvious choice in France.

As we have pointed out already, the services of a good solicitor are important and are therefore equally important when buying a property overseas. The last thing you want is to sign a contract only to find that you are liable for any outstanding service charges or even loan repayments attaching to the property. It may sound improbable, but it happens a lot to British homeowners who are so anxious to secure what they see as a dream home that they forget to make the most basic enquiries. You can use your local solicitor to buy a foreign property, but it might be better to use one who has experience of dealing with other countries. Get in touch with the Law Society in London, which has a list of solicitors who specialise in overseas property deals.

Wherever possible, try to deal with firms that have some representation in the UK. There are plenty of well known firms such as Bovis and Wimpey actively developing on the Continent, and the large British estate agency firms sell properties all over the world. If you are in any doubt about a firm of developers or 'agents', contact the Institute of Foreign Property Owners, who will be able to verify whether the property and the person offering it are genuine. The IFPO is a good place to start because it also has a comprehensive list of UK companies offering property in the region of your choice.

Timesharing

Unless you are rich enough that you can afford a private jet to fly you to your alpine apartment every weekend, your second home is really only going to be used as an occasional holiday home. Timesharing offers a practical and financially rewarding solution to this situation. What you are getting for your money is a holiday apartment or villa reserved for you at certain times of the year for a given number of years. You pay a few thousand pounds for this, and if the area is a popular one, you should see a return on your original investment if you decide to sell your share at some future time. While you own it, you will be required to contribute towards the annual cost of maintenance, insurance and rates, but as (it is to be hoped) you are only one of many owners, the contributions should be small.

Timesharing is very popular. In Britain there are at least 100,000 families who own their share of a dream villa. There are timeshares all over the world, including the Lake District and the Scottish Highlands for those who prefer to stay in Britain. The flexibility of a timeshare extends to being able to swap time with other owners, possibly in different countries. All the major UK developers such as Barratt, Wimpey, European Ferries and Kenning Atlantic operate an exchange network. There are also two American firms, Resort Condominiums International and Interval International, who for a nominal fee will put you in touch with exchange partners in the area of your choice.

Problems

Not all timeshares are a good investment, which is why potential buyers should not throw caution to the winds. The timeshare business has been given a bad name by unscrupulous developers who employ high pressure salesmen to get unsuspecting people to hand over deposits on properties they haven't even seen. If you are offered gifts and incentives to buy a timeshare, ask yourself why they have to try so hard. Is the property in a poor location? Is it even built yet?

It was to improve this image that some of the largest UK timeshare developers (including Barratt and Wimpey) formed the Timeshare Developers Group. This group was set up to introduce measures for consumer protection including a cooling off period of five working days to give the buyer a chance to reconsider. However, this group subsequently came together with the British Property Timeshare Association and the European Holiday Timeshare Association to form a single trade association of the British based timeshare industry, the Timeshare Developers Association. All members are now scrutinised to ensure they have a strong financial base and that they adhere to detailed legal requirements.

If you purchase your timeshare through members of the Association, you may feel that this is sufficient protection and that you shouldn't need to undertake any detailed investigation. Nevertheless, the Office of Fair Trading offers the more general message of, 'Don't rush into anything' and offers the following guidelines:

1 Sign nothing at a first meeting.
2 Pay nothing at a first meeting.
3 Ignore pressure to sign early to obtain a discount.
4 Ignore offers of gifts or incentives.
5 Demand full written details of what you're being offered.
6 Ask a solicitor to look at the contract.
7 Be especially careful about timeshare deals offered when you are on holiday.

8   Finally, can you really afford it?

There may ultimately be nothing wrong with the deal you are offered, but don't take the chance. Only deal with firms that are registered with the Department of Trade & Industry in the United Kingdom (there are plenty to choose from) and don't forget to do the things you would do if you were buying a property in this country. See the property, get to know the area, and if possible, try to meet someone else who owns a share of the same property. As long as you are under no illusions about what you are getting there is no reason why you shouldn't get maximum enjoyment and financial reward from a timeshare.

Sale and leaseback

This is becoming a popular alternative to the timeshare idea. Basically, you buy the whole property and then lease it back to a developer or agent who lets it out. Thus you tackle the problem of having the place empty for months at a time, while getting the full benefit of any capital appreciation in the property. With sale and leaseback you have greater choice with regard to your allotted time plus the same flexibility as a timeshare to exchange weeks with other resorts. The properties are invariably offered at discount prices and there are no recurring charges to pay in the early years.

Raising the money

Loans for the purchase of property overseas are available from foreign banks. They will lend maybe 50% of the purchase price at a higher rate of interest than you would be charged by a UK bank (around 20%) and most of them expect full repayment within ten years. You should always get competent professional advise before arranging a loan with an overseas bank

Some UK lenders are willing to grant loans for second homes overseas. The typical loan will have an interest rate higher than for UK property but lower than those charged by foreign banks. You will normally be granted a loan representing 80% of valuation, repayable over 20 years.

Alternatively, you could raise some cash against the value of your first home. Bear in mind that you can only use the free equity of your property (its current value minus your outstanding mortgage) as collateral for a new loan.

A company director or key executive may also be able to make use of the loanback facility in his executive pension plan. This allows you to unlock the capital in your pension and is available on most regular premium pension contracts. This option does ultimately reduce your pension benefits so it should not be entered into lightly. If you are not sure about it, ask your financial adviser for guidance.

Extra insurance needs

It is not possible to extend your UK house insurance to cover a second property overseas. You will need to make separate arrangements for insuring your second home and its contents. If it is an apartment in a block, then you will simply pay a share of the block policy as a maintenance charge and then all you have to do is insure the contents. A number of UK insurance companies offer cover on foreign properties, or alternatively you can use a foreign insurer. The majority of people buying on resale will simply continue with the insurance company that has been insuring it previously. The premiums can be expensive, especially if the apartment is standing empty for months at a time or if you intend to let it out to strangers.

Useful contacts

The Institute of Foreign Property Owners – Tel: 01–323 1225
Timeshare Developers Association: Tel: 01–821 8845
Osbornes (overseas property agents) Tel: 01–485 8811

9 Home and business

Running a business from home has some fairly major advantages over the alternatives. You don't have to pay any additional rent or mortgage, the cost of services is tax deductible and you don't waste time travelling to and from an office.

As long as you are not disturbing anyone or breaking any bye-laws, building regulations or covenants you are perfectly at liberty to use your home as an office or the base for a small business. If you are a leaseholder, it is necessary to check the terms of your lease to make sure there is no specific rule against carrying on a business on the premises. If you think of it while you are buying your home, ask your solicitor to make you aware of any local authority restrictions on business conducted from home.

Running a business from home

Naturally, if you are using your home as a business base, you should consider the tax treatment of such activity, particularly if you are self-employed and this is your actual 'place of business'. If you have set up a limited company, your registered office should be your home address, which is all the proof the tax office needs that this is, in fact, your real place of business.

Working from home means that you can claim for some household expenses as allowable for income tax purposes.

These include a proportion of normal household outgoings such as rates, lighting, heating, telephone, cleaning and insurance. Travelling expenses incurred entirely in connection with your business are also still allowable.

The tax position

If you are buying your home with a view to working from it (for yourself), you may be able to claim additional relief on your mortgage payments, over and above £30,000. Clear cut cases include shops with flats above and houses with 'surgery' extensions.

Using part of your home for your work gives rise to a potential capital gains tax charge when you come to sell. To give you an idea of how much you might be liable for, assume that when you sell you have made a net gain (after allowable costs and CGT indexation) of £30,000. If there were six rooms in your house and one was used exclusively for work, one sixth of your gain (ie £5,000) would be potentially chargeable to CGT. You can claim 'rollover' relief however, if you reinvest the proceeds of the sale in another property, part of which is again used for your profession.

If you are over 60 and you sell your home, part of which has been used for business, you are eligible for retirement relief on the first £125,000 and 50% of any additional capital gains between £125,000 and £500,000. The actual amount of relief you receive is calculated according to how many years in the last ten you have operated from home in this way.

Office premises

Looking for suitable business premises apart from your home is the same process. Do as much enquiring and viewing as you can. The larger firms of estate agents should have details of commercial properties in the area. Your local government office may have some useful information on properties

available and also on grants or subsidies for which you may
be eligible. There are also many regional development
agencies, specifically created to encourage small businesses
in various parts of the country. These include enterprise
zones, industrial space available in run-down areas, which
are free of any restrictions on planning. The best way to locate
the enterprise agency for your region is to contact the
Department of Trade and Industry or the small firms advisory
service run by the Department of Employment.

Buying and running business premises frees you from dealing
with a landlord whose only interest might be how much rent
he can squeeze out of you. But it still involves you in the
same responsibilities you assume with a house or flat, and
more. The additional cost of furniture, machinery, insurance
and basic services must all be taken into account. You must
be sure that you can make enough money out of the business
to pay off any loan you may take out. Plus you have to make
sure that you abide by health and safety regulations, and the
town planning regulations. Your solicitor should make sure
that the building is registered as business premises, that there
are no restrictions on the hours you can work there or the
amount of noise you can make, and that planning permission
will not be withheld for any structural changes you may
want to make.

Another thing to bear in mind is the location. Is it practical
for your business to be in the middle of an industrial
wasteland with no amenities and poor access to major road
and rail services just because the site is cheap?

The alternative is to lease the premises, which means you
don't have to find so much money up front, but at the same
time, you don't get any return on your money. Use an estate
agent you feel has your best interests at heart and let him
handle all the negotiations for you, including, if you wish,
negotiating your rent for you.

Using the equity in your home

If the business cannot be run from your home, the search for
premises will, it is to be hoped, be part of a more detailed
costing of your affairs. The golden rule for success as a small
businessman is to get your costings and your cash flow
forecasts right. When it comes to raising the money, you may
decide to borrow against your existing assets such as your
house, your life assurance policy if you have one, and any
valuables you may possess. Bear in mind when estimating
how much you can borrow, that a lender will only be willing
to grant you a percentage of their value.

For example, say you have had your house valued at £80,000
and you still have £30,000 worth of mortgage repayments
outstanding. You can only borrow against the £50,000 worth
of free equity but you won't be offered the full amount.
Expect to be offered in the region of £40,000, assuming
property prices are stable.

The rules of letting

In the event that you decide to raise some extra income by
letting the property, you should make yourself fully aware
of the law and where you stand as a would-be landlord.
Contact your solicitor and ask him to brief you on the Rent
Acts, or visit your local Citizens Advice Bureau. The CAB
will have up to date leaflets that weigh up the pros and cons
of being a landlord. The leaflets are issued by the Department
of the Environment and are called *Letting Rooms in Your
Home, Letting Your Home or Retirement Home* and *The Rent
Acts and You.*

The taxation of holiday letting

Until the Finance Act 1984, the Inland Revenue was not convinced that landlords were running a business and that their profits should be treated as unearned income. But since 1984, tax relief has been granted on the basis that commercial letting of holiday accommodation is a 'trade'.

Income tax

To qualify for relief on such income, the property has to be available on a holiday let for at least 140 days a year and it must be occupied for at least 70 days in that year. In addition, the rules stipulate that during a seven month period, the accommodation should not be occupied by the same tenant for more than 31 days at a time.

Where the landlord is married and the wife has no other earnings, it is particularly tax efficient if the lettings business is run by her as she will then qualify for the wife's earnings allowance. However, this can get complicated and depends on the wife's precise financial relationship with her husband, the landlord.

The Inland Revenue also allows various expenses such as the provision of furniture, plus the cost of repairs, to be deductible against letting income. A 10% deduction from the annual rent, less any rates is the common method of calculation. Also deductible is any interest paid on a loan for buying or improving holiday accommodation. And any losses you may make in this business are offsettable against income from elsewhere.

As your holiday letting profits qualify as 'relevant earnings' you can put up to 17.5% of the money into a pension scheme which is a particularly tax efficient way of saving out of your pre-tax income. In some cases you are allowed to carry the tax relief back one year if you elect to pay the premiums before the following 5 April.

Capital gains tax

Rollover relief is available on the sale of property used for business purposes. This means that there will be no liability to CGT as long as you acquire a replacement property which is put to the same use.

When you finally dispose of your holiday let property, you may qualify for retirement relief, which is available on the first £125,000 and 50% of any capital gains between £125,000 and £500,000. You must be at least 60 years old to qualify. You are not allowed to stop using the property for business and reverting to using it for personal needs.

Under the Rent Act, landlords letting their own home or retirement home, and servicemen letting a home intended for their own future use, have what is called 'mandatory' or guaranteed right of repossession. This means that if the tenant does not leave when the agreement ends, and the landlord has to apply for a court order, the court must grant the landlord a possession order, provided all the necessary conditions have been fulfilled.

Local authority short term housing offers a solution to the problems of restricted contracts. Under the Housing Act 1985, local authorities are allowed to lease for short periods, usually two years. You have the place valued and the rent is set according to current market rates. This is paid to you quarterly in advance. The council lets the rooms out to homeless families as licensees (not tenants) which means it can guarantee you vacant possession at the end of the term. In the meantime, your only responsibility is for the rates and water rates, plus a share of any repair bills.

Useful contacts

Department of Employment (Small Firms Service) –
Tel: 01–730 8451
Department of the Environment – Tel: 01–212 3434

10 Housing for older people

As the population ages, the problems of housing for older people become greater. At the turn of the century, 5% of the population could be classed as 'elderly' (ie over the age of 65). Today, 15 per cent of the population fits into that category, with an increasing number of people in their 70s and 80s. Old age in itself is not the problem – increasing years don't necessarily mean that you lose your wits. But the need to reconsider your living accommodation may be a necessity because old age does bring frailty and the need to provide more easily manageable accommodation.

Moving to a smaller house

Whether you should move or stay put is a question which only you can answer. It may seem quite sensible for a couple in their 60s to leave their large house and equally large garden and buy a small two-bedroomed bungalow on the basis that it is an insurance against reaching their 80s and not being quite so lively. There is an obvious logic to that but no more than, say, another pair who decide to remain in their family home because reaching old age doesn't necessarily mean that they have to sacrifice space.

The decision is yours but any accommodation should be so arranged that it's easy and convenient to run. If you decide to stay in your present home, you should look at it to see if it can be re-arranged in ways that are compatible with growing older. One approach is to try and envisage everything likely to go wrong during later years and then equip your house accordingly for instance:

- If a long illness or some disability is a likely possibility, is there a downstairs room that could be switched to use as a bedroom?
- Are there facilities which would let you live without undue strain on the ground floor?
- Have you got easy access to the garden and the house, a kitchen with cupboards within easy reach with undemanding equipment and storage space?
- Is the home heating and insulation of a high standard?
- Is the lighting adequate ie have you abolished all those dark patches?
- Are there grab rails in the shower room and bathroom, lever taps instead of the turn variety, a good security system for doors and windows?

Getting older isn't necessarily a reason for moving – it may be perfectly sensible (and possibly even cheaper) to adapt your existing house to your later years. But if you do decide to move, the solution is to move when it's easy. You may be reluctant to leave the family home but it's better to move to a smaller house while you still have the stamina to cope with the hassle. Moving house in your late 60s could be a wrench while moving in your late 70s could be traumatic.

Sheltered housing

Sheltered housing is usually explained as grouped housing for elderly people who, while living their own independent life in their own self-contained units, may be vulnerable because of their age and require some degree of care supplied by a warden. The warden's job is to keep an unobtrusive and friendly eye on residents and to respond to an emergency signal for help.

There has been a transformation in the sheltered housing market in recent years. The main influence at work is the private construction industry as builders have discovered that a new and expanding market for the supply of purpose-built dwellings for elderly people, normally home owners, has come into existence. Today, there are many developments of grouped housing available to anyone, and normally on a leasehold basis. All levels of the market are catered for from country houses (eg Country Houses Association Limited) to village-type retirement communities and purpose-built blocks of flats. Basically, the emphasis is on accommodation providing one or two bedrooms.

Although the appeal is to older people, there are increasing numbers of younger retired people who are beginning to opt for this type of housing. To them, sheltered housing provides a trouble-free home with the assurance that the accommodation is eminently suitable not only now but for when they grow older.

If you are interested in grouped housing then you should satisfy yourself on a number of points:

- Is the property freely marketable – provided that the purchaser is of the required age (the age of entry to this kind of housing is usually from 55 or 60 onwards)?
- Does the leaseholder retain the right to sell the residence himself and what proceeds, if any, are deducted from the selling price?
- Is there an obligation to contribute towards a 'sinking fund' for major repairs?
- What is the length of the lease?
- What is the amount of ground rent?

With sheltered housing you will normally be expected to pay a service charge and this should cover all outside repairs and maintenance, the upkeep of gardens, estate lighting, property insurance and the maintenance of the alarm system as well as the cost of warden service. You should check to see if there are any extra costs and also (most important) check on what the arrangements are for increasing this charge.

Finally, check on the overall management of the housing complex. Builders often enter into an agreement with a housing association so that the latter eventually becomes responsible for the administration and running of the scheme. Such organisations have often had a long experience of specialised housing for older people and the link is of mutual benefit.

For straightforward house-hunting in a particular area, there's no particular mystique although you might find that the Citizens Advice Bureau has information for you. Details of builders engaged in this kind of housing can be obtained from the New Homes Marketing Board, Tel: 01–580 5588.

The Housing Information Department of Age Concern, Tel: 01–640 5431 issues a buyers guide to sheltered housing. Age Concern can also supply information on housing provided by local authorities and housing associations.

Home income plans

Many older people are in a much worse financial situation today than they were a few years ago, especially if they are living on a fixed income. Even with the relatively modest increase in inflation that we've seen over the last few years, an increasing amount of money is needed to maintain a standard of living. The temptation is to spend savings but if you do, you are sacrificing some of your income that these savings will provide in the future. The position becomes worse if we don't look far enough ahead because people today are living longer than ever before. For example, a woman of 75 has a life expectancy of 12 years which in fact means that she has a 50–50 chance of living beyond the age of 87. It's important for people in this position to think carefully about their future.

If you own your house or flat you have a very valuable asset but it represents capital that is tied up at a time when you may need extra spendable income. You may also find that your home, your biggest financial asset, is also becoming your greatest liability as the cost of maintaining it eats into your pensions or savings.

A solution to the problem is through a home income plan offered by one or two insurance companies and building societies. The plan is designed to offer elderly homeowners an immediate increase in income for the rest of their lives. In some cases, where a cash lump sum is an essential requirement, this too can be arranged.

How they work

The plan involves a mortgage linked to an annuity, but where you still retain the ownership of your own home. The insurance company lends you up to 80% of the value of your house or flat with a current maximum loan of £30,000. This is used to buy an annuity which will be paid to you for the rest of your life. Part of it pays the fixed interest on the mortgage with the balance being paid into your bank account each month. There is an additional benefit which can boost the net value of your plan quite considerably. The interest on the loan also qualifies for tax relief which means that only 75% of the mortgage interest is actually deducted from the annuity income, whether you pay tax or not.

Loans of up to 80% of the value of the property are normally available providing it is leased freehold or has a sufficient lease remaining. Up to 10% of the loan can be taken as a cash sum which could be particularly useful if there are improvements or repairs required to the property. A big advantage of home income plans is that it is often possible to go back to the lender for further loans as the value of the property appreciates. In this way, your income can be topped-up from time to time (subject, of course, to the total loan not exceeding £30,000).

The loan is repayable on the death of the planholder out of the proceeds of selling the house which means that any heirs will have to forgo inheriting this amount. They will, however, still inherit the portion not covered by the loan and any subsequent increase in value.

The total amount of income received will be different according to your age, your tax position and the value of your house. Anybody considering a home income plan should *always* discuss it with their solicitor or other professional adviser and it also makes a lot of sense to involve the members of your immediate family (as they could be losing some of their inheritance).

One type of home income plan which is not particularly recommended is a home reversion scheme. This involves not mortgaging the house but selling it outright. You still retain the right to live in your house for life but inevitably this means that the price paid for the property will be below its market value. The apparent advantage of the scheme to you is that you can keep the whole of the annuity payment as there will be no mortgage interest to pay. The major disadvantage is that both you and your heirs lose the benefit of any further increases in the value of the property. You will also be responsible for maintaining the house including any necessary repairs.

11 Problems and what to do about them

Despite all the planning and professional guidance, unexpected problems can arise. There can be a tendency to nurse problems and to keep them to yourself, when in fact people are usually very willing to help you if you have a problem. Indeed, there are many organisations specifically aimed at helping others.

If you can't afford the mortgage repayments

No one should expect to have much spare cash immediately after buying a property. If you have followed the guidelines in previous chapters you should be fully appraised of the true cost of buying and be able to budget accordingly. Nevertheless, some of you will inevitably have trouble meeting the monthly mortgage payments at some time. You may be sacked from your job, taken seriously ill, or even disabled.

Those who have taken out some insurance to cover the mortgage payments in the event of sickness or disability will not have to worry on that score. If your income falls dramatically and you are not covered by a mortgage protection policy, you may be entitled to some support from social security. Your local DHSS or Citizens Advice Bureau will have full details.

Whatever the reason, if you get into financial trouble, let your building society, bank or insurance company know. Do it as soon as you realise just how poor you are and the lender will try to work something out that will make the payments easier. Extending the mortgage term or simply reducing the initial repayments are two solutions which they can offer you. Honesty is the best policy. If you try to pull the wool over their eyes by skipping payments while claiming there is nothing wrong, you risk being repossessed and you will certainly spoil your chances of ever raising a mortgage again.

Problems with new property

Although it is fair to assume that a brand new property will need less repair than an old one, you may experience the odd cracked wall in your newly built home. Most properties have some 'give' built into them and start to reveal cracks as they begin to settle. If you are at all concerned about this, contact the developer and ask to have it fixed. Ninety-nine % of newly built properties are covered by a National House Building Council certificate. If any structural defects appear within the first two years after the certificate has been granted, it is the builder's responsibility to put these right free of charge. Between the third and tenth years, you are protected against damage due to any 'major' structural defects such as dry rot, subsidence, chemical failure of materials or a collapsing roof. This is a protection against catastrophe; it does not include cover for ordinary repairs or for 'minor' structural defects. There has to be actual damage. Also excluded are wet rot or any defects due to negligence on the part of the house owner, storm damage or any risks covered by a householder's insurance policy. If you do not receive your NHBC certificate, you are entitled to sue the vendor for its absence.

In 1983, the NHBC introduced a warranty for flat conversions. The scheme was modelled on the new homes warranty, but the cover is for six years rather than ten with the builder being responsible for the first year only. The conversions scheme differs, however, from the new homes warranty in that it is entirely voluntary. Builders apply for the warranty on whichever properties they choose (provided they contain at least three units and are no more than four storeys and a basement high).

What is important to remember is that the NHBC are not going to react to a sudden request for help or a phone call. They will wish to make quite sure that you have a legitimate problem and so it is important to write to them describing the problem in detail. Make sure that all the negotiations between you and the builder are in writing and that you keep copies of all correspondence in order that you have everything you need when you make a claim.

Also, bear in mind that the NHBC is concerned only with structural problems affecting the property ie questions of whether the property has been correctly constructed from a technical point of view. If you commission a builder to build your house for you and he dosen't deliver the house he promised, then that is a contractual matter between you and the builder and you will have to take legal action against the builder for breach of contract. You should consult your solicitor on this—the NHBC will not be able to get involved.

Problems with solicitors

It is not unknown for housebuyers to experience problems with their solicitor, particularly with regard to the solicitor's failure to process the sale on time. To deal with complaints from dissatisfied buyers, the Law Society has set up a Solicitors Complaints Bureau. If you have a complaint you would like to make, you should write to the SCB, clearly stating why you are dissatisfied. The SCB will then investigate the solicitors's conduct, which will include asking him for his comments on your letter. His reply will be sent to you together with the SCB's comments, and you will be told whether any further action is going to be taken.

Complaints against surveyors

If you discover a major structural defect that has gone undetected by your surveyor, you may be able to take this up with the Royal Institution of Chartered Surveyors, although this is unlikely to prove satisfactory to you. Obviously, the RICS will only deal with members of the Institution and their powers are limited to matters of delay in processing your survey and failure to disclose any conflict of interest. They cannot investigate disputes and they have no power to award compensation. So in a case of alleged professional negligence, the best course of action would be to consult a solicitor or your local Citizens Advice Bureau.

Complaints against estate agents

Contrary to what you might believe, estate agents are subject to a variety of rules and regulations, principally by the Estate Agents Act 1979, but also by the National Association of Estate Agents and the Incorporated Society of Valuers and Auctioneers. If you have a complaint against an estate agent (which applies in the main to sellers rather than buyers) get in touch with the NAEA. They will investigate your case and, if a breach of their code of conduct is discovered, a disciplinary sub-committee will hold court. Should the committee find in favour of the complainant, the agent will be fined or suspended. In 1987, there were apparently 11 such cases heard, all but two of which found in favour of the complainant.

The Associations are unable to deal with disputes over

commission, however. These must be dealt with by the courts, so if you are in dispute with an agent over commission, contact a solicitor.

Trouble with your neighbours

If one of your neighbours is constantly giving wild parties till the wee small hours, you have grounds for complaint. But what do you do? Before you declare outright war, try to reason with them. If you live in a block of flats and the lease specifies noise restrictions, bring this to your neighbour's attention.

If they refuse to see reason and you cannot reach any form of compromise, your only alternative is to seek a court order or a local authority abatement notice. The legal view is that if your neighbour is preventing you from living peacefully in your own home, then he is committing a nuisance.

This may not be so easy to prove, however, because everyone has a different idea about what constitutes disruption. To assist your legal advisers in establishing a case, make a note of every disturbance, when it occurred and how long for. If you can get another neighbour to corroborate your story, you have a stronger case.

For further information on your rights, visit your local Citizens Advice Bureau and ask for a copy of the Department of the Environment leaflet, *Bothered by Noises*

Leasehold problems

To avoid the situation where you cannot sell your property because it has a short lease, do not buy anything with less than 60 years left to run on the lease, preferably more. As it is, most lenders won't even consider a mortgage on a leasehold property with less than 60 years to run.

The only situation where you should buy a property that has only a few years to go before the lease runs out is if you have the option of buying the freehold. In which case, you can renegotiate the lease when it expires.

Although you are bound by the terms of your lease to pay recurring fees such as ground rent and service charges, if you feel you are being overcharged you do have the right to ask how the fees are calculated. Ground rent is usually a nominal charge that doesn't vary from year to year. But the service charges are at the discretion of the landlord or freeholder and should be based on the costs of maintaining the building, including any special work that needs to be done. You are entitled to see how the charges were arrived at.

Gazumping

Britain is lagging behind in legislating to cut down on the amount of gazumping that goes on in the residential property market. As it stands, house buyers are increasingly at the mercy of the cash rich property buyer who comes in with a late bid that forces the seller to renege on his original deal. That said, there are just as many deals that fall through because the buyer gets cold feet as there are instances of gazumping.

There is no surefire solution to this problem. The best advice if you want to avoid being gazumped is to buy out of season, ie in mid-winter when your competitors are off skiing. And offer to pay the asking price. That way you are at least cutting down the risk of disappointment.

For sellers, the advice is to get the price right to begin with and if you feel that price is reasonable, stick to it and don't allow yourself to be knocked down. You won't be so inclined to gazump if you get what you are asking for the property.

The Government and the legal profession have both put forward proposals to try to improve the situation. The Law Commission has suggested that a voluntary payment of 0.5% of the agreed price be deposited with the vendor's solicitor before the exchange of contracts as a measure of each side's commitment to the deal. Should it fail to go through within four weeks, the innocent party gets the money, unless there is a valid reason for the delay.

Useful contact

National Consumer Council – Tel: 01–730 3469

12 Checklists

This book has covered a lot of ground so you should now be far more aware of the various steps and who's who in the house buying process. The following checklists will act as an aide-memoire as you go about your house hunting.

How to choose your home

1 List your requirements:
   (a) number of rooms;
   (b) proximity to local amenities, shops, school and transport;
   (c) parking facilities.
2 Prepare a budget taking into account all the incidental expenses involved, what size of mortgage can you raise and comfortably pay off every month?
3 Decide on an area; assuming that you haven't already decided where you want to live, investigate the areas you think you can afford.
4 Contact estate agents in the area; they will send you details of properties in your price range.
5 Check newspapers and magazines; local papers always have plenty of property for sale. The quality Sunday papers often have property for sale privately in the small ads. And for those with enough money, there is *Country Life* and the free property magazines that circulate in the more affluent areas.
6 Visit a number of different properties; this will give you

a feel for the general quality of property in an area. It will also give you an education in estate agency jargon.

7 If in doubt, go back; don't allow yourself to be rushed around a property. If you decide you like a particular place, but you have reservations, go away and think about it. Make a list of your reservations and when you go back try to visit at a different time of day.

Services you may need straight away

Don't expect to find that everything is working perfectly when you move in. Let's assume the worst. The previous occupant didn't pay his electricity bill, which means you will have no light, no heat and no hot water. You try phoning the electricity board but your vendor hasn't paid his telephone bill either.

To avoid this scenario, you should attempt to find out exactly what state the property is going to be in when you take possession of it. If your vendor appears trustworthy, you can simply ask him or her about the state of the telephone, electricity, gas (if any), water and plumbing. Bear in mind also that British Telecom, the gas and electricity boards all have waiting lists for repairs and maintenance, so you could be waiting weeks for essential services if you leave it until you move in.

Telling people you are moving

You will obviously think to tell your friends and relations that you are moving but there are many other people who will need to know that you have changed address. Some of the people you will need to tell are:

- Bank
- Building society
- Stock and bonds
- Post Office
- Local authority

- Employer
- Inland Revenue
- DHSS

- AA/RAC
- Vehicle Licensing Office
- Insurance companies

- Book clubs
- Mail order catalogues
- Clubs and associations etc

Glossary of housebuying terms

Absolute title Most properties are registered in 'title absolute' which means that a property passes completely and absolutely to whoever buys it. There is no better title to registered land than title absolute.

Annual percentage rate (APR) This is the true rate of interest that you will pay on a loan.

Apportionment The calculation of how much of the annual rates bill is owed by the vendor and how much by the buyer.

Assignment A transfer of ownership of property (particularly leasehold) from one person to another.

Auction Property can be sold at auction, the same way as antiques and famous paintings. Large and historic houses are often sold this way.

Beneficial owner An alternative term for absolute owner.

Bridging loan A short term bank loan at a higher rate of interest than normal.

Capital gains tax (CGT) When selling a second home you may well be liable to this tax being charged on the net profit which you make from the sale.

Capital and interest The two elements of a mortgage. The capital (the amount you are borrowing) remains fixed while the interest varies with the level of interest rates in general.

Chain You are waiting to complete on a sale in order to buy, and the person you are selling to is waiting to complete his sale to buy your property, and so on and so on. All it takes is for one link in the chain to break and everybody is affected.

Collateral Property or other asset used as a guarantee for a loan.

Completion When the transfer of ownership is signed, sealed and delivered, and you get to pick up the keys.

Contract The contract retains all the important details of the property transaction, the terms of which must be agreed by both sides before your solicitor can proceed with the transfer of title.

Conversion Where a large house has been split up into a number of separate flats.

Conveyancing The legal process involved in buying and selling property.

Covenants Rules and regulations of a property contained in its lease.

Delivery Handing over the deeds to a property and therefore finally transferring the ownership of the property.

Disbursements The extra costs, such as stamp duty, land registry fees and insurance, that are met by your solicitor and passed onto you when he presents his final bill.

Endowment mortgage A loan to buy a property which will be repaid out of the maturity value of a life assurance endowment policy.

Equity The value of the property which is not mortgaged nor has any other loans outstanding against it ie your part of the house.

Exchange of contracts Once there are no more questions and terms have been agreed, contracts are exchanged, at which point both buyer and seller are bound to the deal.

Fee simple Another term for freehold.

Freehold If you are the freeholder, you own the property outright, regardless of the length of your lease. Freehold property is therefore worth more than leasehold.

Gazumping An infuriating symptom of the laws of supply and demand. You have been gazumped if, after having your offer accepted, the seller receives and accepts a higher bid.

Ground rent A nominal annual charge for leaseholders, usually no more than £100.

Inspection fee The lender's fee for sending someone to inspect the property you propose to buy with their money. Fees vary according to the lender and the size of the property.

Land Registry fee Part of the conveyancing process registering the transfer of ownership, for which there is a fee. It is usually only a few pounds.

Leasehold The majority of flats are leasehold properties, which means that you own the place itself, but not the land on which it is built. Once the lease runs out, ownership reverts to whoever owns the freehold.

Lessee The owner of the lease. The relationship between the freeholder and the lessee is the same as between landlord and tenant.

Lessor The person granting a lease.

MIRAS Stands for Mortgage Interest Relief At Source, which probably makes it as clear as mud. The first bit (MIR) is the discount you get on the interest payments of your mortgage, based on your income tax rate. So as a basic rate taxpayer, you get a 25% discount on your interest payments. The second bit (AS) refers to the fact that this is taken into account in your pay packet.

Mortgage A loan for which a property is the security.

Mortgagee The person or organisation, bank, building society, finance house which is lending the money.

Mortgagor The person who is borrowing the money.

Part possession Tends to complicate matters unduly as you are basically moving into one part of a house while there are tenants in the remainder. So although you may be able to get rent from the other people, you are also responsible for maintaining that part of the property that you don't live in. You are also stuck with people you may not get on with. Not surprisingly, the major lenders won't grant mortgages on properties with part possession.

Pension mortgage A loan to buy a property which will be repaid out of the cash lump sum at pension age.

Purpose-built Relates to flats which were built as flats rather than converted within a house. The advantage of a purpose of a purpose-built flat over a conversion is that it probably has solid walls, but conversions tend to be more popular because they often have larger rooms.

Rateable value Your local council's assessment of how much rates you should pay according to the size of your property and the services it receives in relation to all the other properties in your area.

Redemption The final paying off of a mortgage.

Registered land Property whose full details are filed with the Land Registry. The registry was established to hold the authenticated details of all UK properties. But, unfortunately, there are still many that are not registered. If the place you are buying is not registered, your solicitor should make sure that the title deeds are authentic before any exchange takes place.

Repayment mortgage A loan to purchase a house which is repaid with regular payments of both capital and interest throughout its repayment period.

Requisitions on title Questions that your solicitor has about the vendor's title deeds are sent to the vendor's solicitor, and they are called requisitions on title.

Restrictive covenant Restrictions for the purposes to which you may put the land you have purchased.

Scale fee A fee charged from a standard list of fees based upon the price being paid for a property, usually by solicitors and estate agents.

Stamp duty An Inland Revenue tax currently at the rate of 1% of the purchase price of the property, if this exceeds £30,000.

Subject to contract A 'gentleman's agreement' that a property is sold. However, both the buyer and the seller may pull out of this position without any legal or financial penalty.

Survey A surveyor's report on the condition of a property.

Tenant Someone who pays rent to live in a property which he does not own.

Tenure A term for the type of ownership of property eg leasehold, freehold.

Vacant possession The contract between yourself and the vendor should state when you can take vacant possession of the property. Or in other words, when will the place be empty for you to move in.

Valuation An assessment of the property's value made by either the estate agent or the mortgage lender.

Vendor The person selling the property.

Useful addresses

Age Concern
Housing Information Dept.
16 Pitcairn Road
MITCHAM
Surrey
CR4 3LL

Tel: 01–640 5431

Association of British
Insurers
Aldermary House
10–15 Queen Street
LONDON
EC4N 1TT

Tel: 01–248 4477

British Association of
Removers
279 Grays Inn Road
LONDON
WC1 8SY

Tel: 01–837 3088

Building Societies
Association
3 Savile Row
LONDON
W1X 1AF

Tel: 01–437 0655

Citizens Advice Bureau
136–44 City Road
LONDON
EC1V 2QN

Tel: 01–251 2000

Consumers Association
14 Buckingham Street
LONDON
WC2N 6DS

Tel: 01–839 1222

Country Houses Association
41 Kingsway
LONDON
WC2B 6UB

Tel: 01–836 1624

Department of Employment
(Small Firms Service)
Ebury Bridge House
2–18 Ebury Bridge Road
LONDON
SW1W 8QD

Tel: 01–730 8451

Department of the
Environment
(Homeloan Schemes)
2 Marsham Street
LONDON
SW1P 3EB

Tel: 01–212 3434

Federation of Master
Builders
Gordon Fisher House
33 John Street
LONDON WC1

Tel: 01–242 7583

House Builders Federation
82 New Cavendish Street
LONDON
W1M 8AD

Tel: 01–580 5588

House Building Advisory
Bureau
10 Bolt Court
Fleet Street
LONDON
EC4A 3DB

Tel: 01–583 0518

Housing Corporation
149 Tottenham Court Road
LONDON
W1P 0BN

Tel: 01–387 9466

Incorporated Society of
Valuers and Auctioneers
3 Cadogan Gate
LONDON
SW1X 0AS

Tel: 01–235 2282

Institute of Foreign
Property Owners
72 Tottenham Court Road
1st Floor
LONDON
W1P 9AP

Tel: 01–323 1225

Law Society
113 Chancery Lane
LONDON
WC2A 1PL

Tel: 01–242 1222

Law Society of Scotland
PO Box 75
26 Drumsheugh Gardens
EDINBURGH
EH3 7YR

Tel: 031–226 7411

London Building Services
26 Store Street
LONDON
WC1E 7BT

Tel: 01–637 1022

National Association of
Conveyancers
2/4 Chichester Rents
Chancery Lane
LONDON
WC2A 1EG

Tel: 01–405 8582

National Association of
Estate Agents
Arbon House
21 Jury Street
WARWICK
CV34 4EH

Tel: 0926 496800

National Consumer Council
20 Grosvernor Gardens
LONDON
SW1W 0DH

Tel: 01–730 3469

National Federation of
Housing Associations
175 Grays Inn Road
LONDON
WC1X 8UP

Tel: 01–278 6571

National House Building
Council
58 Portland Place
LONDON
W1N 4BU

Tel: 01–580 9381

New Homes Marketing
Board
82 New Cavendish Street
LONDON
W1M 8AD

Tel: 01–580 5588

Road Haulage Association
104 New Kings Road
LONDON
SW6 4LN

Tel: 01–736 1183

Royal Institute of British
Architects
Clients Advisory Service
66 Portland Place
LONDON
W1N 4AD

Tel: 01–580 5533

Royal Institution of Chartered
Surveyors
12 Great George Street
Parliament Square
LONDON
SW1P 3AD

Tel: 01–222 7000

Solicitors Complaints Bureau
Stock Exchange
Old Broad Street
LONDON
EC2N 1HP

Tel: 01–834 2288

Timeshare Developers
Association
23 Buckingham Gate
LONDON
SW1E 6LB

Tel: 01-821 8845

Index

Other titles in this series:

Managing Your Finances   Helen Pridham

Planning Your Pension   Tony Reardon

Running Your Own Business   David Williams

Forthcoming titles include:

Your Home in Spain   Per Svensson

Your Home in Portugal   Rosemary de Rougemont

Planning for School Fees   Danby Block &
   (& Paying for Further Education) Amanda Pardoe

Tax for the Self-Employed   David Williams

Investing in Shares   Hugh Pym &
    Nick Kochan

Insurance – Are You Covered?   Mihir Bose

Leaving Your Money Wisely   Tony Foreman